BUDDHA NATURE NOW

Discovering Your Buddha Nature

Henry Landry, LSC, BGT

Bloomington, IN  Milton Keynes, UK

AuthorHouse™
1663 Liberty Drive, Suite 200
Bloomington, IN 47403
www.authorhouse.com
Phone: 1-800-839-8640

AuthorHouse™ UK Ltd.
500 Avebury Boulevard
Central Milton Keynes, MK9 2BE
www.authorhouse.co.uk
Phone: 08001974150

© *2007 Henry Landry, LSC, BGT. All rights reserved.*

No part of this book may be reproduced, stored in a retrieval system, or transmitted by any means without the written permission of the author.

First published by AuthorHouse 6/20/2007

ISBN: 978-1-4259-9914-8 (sc)

Printed in the United States of America
Bloomington, Indiana

This book is printed on acid-free paper.

1] Buddha Teachings   2] Nichiren   3] Inspirational   4] Self Growth.

DISCOVERING YOUR BUDDHA NATURE

Now Is the Time

"*Faith, Joy, Trust & Wisdom*

*The Absolute Freedom of
the Buddha Way*"

"*My heart is filled with Joy
My doubts and regrets are forever ended
I am at rest in real wisdom*"
Roll Two, Chapter Three, Lotus Sutra

Dedications

To You In Search Of Your Spiritual Health

To all members of the *Nichiren Sangha's* who over the years have inspired the revolution of peaceful means with their own personal spiritual journey.

To my daughter Theresa and her brother Bill

Acknowledgments

I wish to thank: Jean Howell my editor and dear friend who also read the manuscript and offered a creative non buddhist critque

To All those who since 1995 have taken "The Buddha's 7 Lessons" inspiring me to put these words together.

To Rev. Takahashi, who first asked me to start the study groups.

And to Nichiren Daishonin, Tien Tai Chi'I, and Gautama Shakyamuni whose spiritual energies flow throughout the universe everyday.

To the Reader ~ I

Discovering Your Buddha Nature ~ Now Is the Time

Life is about this moment.
In reality that is all there is.

After this moment passes it is NOW your past.
Whether you choose to take a few moments to
read the next few lines is in your future.
NOW is the Time of All phenomena.

Why the Buddha-way? It offers a gentle, disciplined,
understanding of the natural way of life. One of
health, happiness, wisdom and so much more.
The Buddha-way is a living philosophy,
a daily practice of spiritual faith.

In exploring the *Discovery of Your Buddha Nature*, you
will be amazed at how a human, the historical Buddha,
Gautama Shakyamuni, with many of the same qualities
of life as us, became a messenger of hope and inspiration.
His enlightened message has carried on for almost 3,000
years, they are truly worthy of respect and consideration.

The Spiritual Journey is a personal One,
congratulations on your seeking spirit!
This is a message for today in the time and space of NOW !

To the Reader ~ II

In the Buddhist tradition today there are many Buddhist Schools and whether they are Lay Organizations, Buddha Centers or Buddha Temples all fall within two major paths, the *Therevada* or the *Mahayana*. The *Therevada* teachings are not untrue, they are the simply the early and incomplete teachings of *Gautama Shakyamuni*.

The *Mahayana* is divided into two schools, the provisional and the whole or complete Dharma as revealed in the *Lotus Sutra,* of the Former Day of the Law.

In the Buddha-way there is the generic and the specific method of practice. The generic is the bumper sticker, the peace march or the taking on a cause we believe in to help make a difference.

The Specific Method is in understanding that we are connected to our universe through the fusion of the Person and the Law. The Specific is the faith, practice and study in the here and NOW, understanding this moment of eternity in which we are a participants. Specifically how the Buddhist philosophy works in our everyday life.

In PART ONE You will find many interesting topics for your consideration enjoyment and research. The specifics in this book will lead us to the *Latter Day of the Law* and the *Mahayana Nichiren* Buddha Tradition.

In PART TWO you will find the *Lotus Contemplations,* along with the Lineage of the historical first earthly Buddha Shakyamuni and more Lotus Blossoms to enjoy.

The Teacher may open the door, but you must walk through, holding on to the knowledge and learning with the *Realization* of your own empowerment and potential enlightenment.

HL

Nam~MyoHo~Renge~Kyo.

Nam~MyoHo~Renge~Kyo.

Discovering Your Buddha Nature
NOW, Is the Time

Nam~MyoHo~Renge~Kyo

**The "getha" given by the Buddha
of our Latter Day of the Law,
*Nichiren Daishonin***

A simple, first meaning of this "getha" or mantra is:

"*Devotion to the eternal, universal, Law, of the Buddha's teachings as contained in the scripture of the* Lotus *Blossom of the Fine Dharma, through the sound of your beautiful voice, originally the voice of the Buddha!*"

Contents:
DISCOVERING YOUR BUDDHA NATURE ©
NOW IS THE TIME
Part ONE:
Seven Sharing Sessions On the Buddha's Teachings
with *Henry Landry*, LSC, BGT, Buddha Ajari

Introduction & Welcome	3

1ST SHARING SESSION

Selection of Time	8
Three Proofs	12
Is Buddha A God? Is God A Buddha?	17
Enlightenment	20
Cause and Effect ~ The Universal Factor	25

2ND SHARING SESSION

Belief In the Mahayana Nichiren School	27
Personal Meditation Needs Answered ~ Personal Prayer	34
Precepts of the Latter Day of the Law	38
Fusion of the Person and the Law	42
Oneness Realization ~ Actuality of the Buddha-way	44
The Lotus Sutra ~ The Whole & *Comple*te Teaching	47

3RD SHARING SESSION

Nirvana	49
The Five In One Meditation	52
Sound Meditation ~ Chanting of Nam ~ Myoho ~ Renge ~ Kyo	55
Meaning of *NAM~MYOHO~RENGE~KYO*	56
The Significance of Buddha *JUZU** Beads	62

4TH SHARING SESSION

Ten Factors ~ How the Universe Works	69
Ten Worlds ~ How the Dharma Wheel of Life Works	73
The Twelve-linked Chain of Causation ~ Harmony or Suffering	78
NOW, *3,000 In One Momentary Life Force* ~~~ Ichinen Sanzen	81

HEALTH Body, Mind & Spirit, the Elements of Earth, Wind, Fire, Water 87

5ᵗʰ Sharing Session

KARMA ~ The Vast Subject	92
Curing Karmic Disease Our Negative Karma	95
Repaying Our Debts of Gratitude & Good Fortune	97
Trinity of Oneness ~~~ More Health	103

6ᵗʰ Sharing Session

Four Virtues ~ True Self, Happiness, Purity, Eternity	106
Meditation ~ On the Sacred Source ~ Gohonzon	109
The Mysteries of Life & Death	112
How Do Earthly Desires Lead To Enlightenment	117

7ᵗʰ Sharing Session

This is the Buddhist Philosophy	119
The Buddha-way of Patience, Empathy, Love & Compassion	121
Kosen Rufu ~ Buddhist Perspective on Peaceful Means	124
Eternal Original Buddha	127

PART ONE

THE BUDDHA'S 7 LESSONS

SEVEN SHARING SESSIONS OF SPECIFIC METHOD FOR THE APPLICATION OF BUDDHIST FAITH, PRACTICE AND STUDY

"The only permanence in our universe and our lives, the only constant is change!"

Introduction & Welcome

Every heart beats to a different vibration, every personality is its own. Life offers One and all challenges, struggles and the need for strength. This is why we call it the *saha* world or world of endurance. This is the cause of why so few humans reach for personal development, true self and their truth within. The Buddhist philosophy teaches that we each have a Buddha nature or a wisdom nature. The Buddha taught so long ago that through faith, practice and study we can become enlightened not only to our spiritual nature, but to our deepest being and motivations that lead us to wisdom and peaceful means; what in the Buddha-way we call enlightenment.

This book is dedicated to the pathways of knowledge, realization, good fortune, health and happiness. Discovering One's Buddha nature is an exciting, wonderful journey about the Dharma [wisdom teachings] Wheel of dynamic living. But, you must know I only repeat what has been "copied, kept, told, received and recited" for some 3,000 years. As the Buddha requests, it is written so that we may have an opportunity to discover and decide whether or not to pursue our Buddha nature. We are reminded, "by creating a fire from the firewood of earthly desires, one can actualize the compassionate fire of the Buddha." In the beginning our Quest may have several doubts, our academic mind wants to throw the ego at our questions about faith, hope and love, so one is stuck in the *"World of Learning."* When one researches, seeks documentary and theoretical proof, one may come closer to non-backsliding and the *"World of Realization."* For many millions of humans this is as close one gets in understanding the eternal, universal Law of Eternal meaning. This is why the Buddha clearly says: "neither men or women of learning, men or women of realization are able to comprehend it [true-self]." *Lotus Sutra* - Roll One, Chapter 2 The meaning here is that we must get beyond the ego and take simple faith as a stepping stone to understanding we are spiritual beings on a human journey, in the discovery of our spiritual nature.

The Buddha promises all desire, all hope, all our quests can be fulfilled by humble faith. Yet, simple is hard for the intellect to grasp. So, we can take heart when in the present Latter Day of the Law, Nichiren Daishonin [1222 - 1285] tells us: *"In judging the relative merit of Buddhist doctrines, I Nichiren, believe that the best standards are those of reason and documentary proof. And even more valuable than reason and documentary proof is the proof of actual fact."*

It is not necessary to know how to play a violin in order to enjoy the music. Living One's *karma* by working through the life's challenges and living a wise, happy life is Discovering Your Buddha Nature.

Buddha Dharma Wheel

Former Day of the Law
Historical Buddha   *G. Shakyamuni*   Time of the Harvest

Middle Day of the Law
Defining Buddha-way   *Tien Tai Chi'I*   Time of Maturing

Latter Day of the Law
Present Age   *Nichiren Daishonin*   Time of Sowing

Nichiren Daishonin
Compassionate Buddha of the Latter Day of the Law

Born a fisherman's son in 1222, he had caring and loving parents. At age 12 he entered *Seicho-ji Temple* for schooling and to study for priesthood. In 1239, as a priest he began going to various Temples to complete his PhD in the Buddha Dharma. In all he studied for twenty years all the various Buddhist teachings, sects, theories, and doctrines. Confirming and realizing how far the various Buddhist schools had gone away from the historical first Buddha's prophecies as contained within the Lotus Sutra, in 1253, he founded his new Buddhist School or Sect. He did this based on the teachings of the Buddha of the Former Day of the Law, *Gautama Shakyamuni* of India. On the Master, Scholar, Teacher and Chinese Priest *T'ien Tai Chi'I's* proof of the correct method and time for the Buddha-way as the complete and whole teaching. And, on the teachings of the Sage of Japan, *Dengyo, 767-822*. On April 28, 1253 Nichiren, chanted *Namu~Myoho~Renge~Kyo* the all inclusive title of the *Lotus Sutra* and declared that all people are capable of attaining the Buddha-way in the here and Now.

He took the name **Nichiren bo**, later attaining the wisdom and enlightenment title.

His name became: **_Nichiren_** ~~ **Sun-Lotus** ~~ **_Daishonin_** ~~ **Great Sage**

Convinced that the Buddhist gods had abandoned his country of *Japan, h*e questioned why his country was in turmoil and realized the times were such that no one was practicing life on the basis of sincere spiritual sustain-ability and correct Buddha practice. *Nichiren* understood that historically, the *Latter Day of the Law* had begun about 220 years earlier and that the ways of the Buddha Dharma of the Former and Middle Day of the Law no longer applied. Following the predictions of the *Lotus Sutra* he realized that the 10,000 year Law of Sowing is the time that All may seek their Buddha nature. From the *Lotus Sutra's* perspective, from *Nichiren's* perspective, Earth is the pure land. We need to protect our environment, taking personal time for the discovery of our Spiritual nature seeking enlightenment in the here and Now. *Nichiren,* desiring to end suffering of all people, inscribed a Mandala, called a *Gohonzon,* an object of profound respect. This offering worthy of the respect of all humans offers visual connection with One's Buddha-self. As his Buddhist Sangha, group of new Priests and followers took root he continued to teach both priests and lay believers that the Way included faith, practice and study. He taught that a fundamental practice was through the sound meditation, or chanting of the all inclusive title of the Buddha's highest teaching, offering a profound gathering place for all humankind.

On October 13, 1282 *Nichiren Daishonin* entered Nirvana

The Buddha - The Law - The Beings

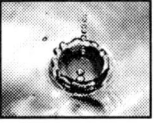

Sharing Session   ONE OF SEVEN

1] The Buddha Way, Who Is Shakyamuni, Who Is Nichiren
2] The Selection of Time, Your Buddha Nature
3] Is Buddha A God, Is God A Buddha
4] Three Proofs of Faith, Practice and Study
5] Meaning of Enlightenment

The goal of Buddhists is to end all suffering, believing that all persons have the inner potential to achieve wisdom and Enlightenment. This idea is the main principle that surrounds the living philosophy of Buddha wisdom. The *Mahayana* Buddha-way is one of the two main streams of Buddhist teachings, considered by academics and theological scholars to be the teachings of *Gautama Shakyamuni's* last dozen or so years. The other, *Theravada* or *Hinyanna,* is composed of the Buddha's first forty years of teachings. The establishment of peaceful means, social harmony and peace beyond boarders politics and cultures, has long been the desire of those who practice the living philosophy of the Buddha Dharma or wisdom teachings.

Buddhists believe the workings of our universe are all subject to a single principle or universal Law. By understanding this universal Law and the manner in which One's potential for wisdom works, a person can unlock the hidden potential within his or her own life, striving to achieve harmony within all three earthly desires, the five lessons, and the seven essentials for good fortune and peaceful means. Once a person becomes awakened to the desires of finding true self, then the first steps of spiritual discovery can begin through a process of study, practice and faith. Naturally, in time, the process is reversed as faith becomes primary and the living philosophy of the Buddha wisdom becomes desirable in One's life.

When we study the Faiths of the world we find much blood. In the name of god and religion people have been tortured, families broken, whole countries plundered and taken over. Also within each and every faith we find much division, break ups, schisms and reforms. We find that because religion is guided by the egos of common mortals it is too often about power, control, money and greed in the name of god. This is the argument most often heard as "god is on our side" or "only our god." Rightfully this misguided concept has caused millions to say I want no part of any religion. In the Buddhist Way there has also been much division and discourse over the thousands of years from one Sect to another, but one article of faith that makes the living philosophy of a Buddha different is it tries to live quietly next to both believers and non-believers offering prayers of peace for All.

Selection of Time

In the *Daiju Sutra* it is noted that the living philosophy of the Buddha-way has three distinct time periods in constant rotation according to the times.

Former Day of the Law   The Buddha-way of the Harvest

Middle Day of the Law   The Buddha-way of Maturing

Latter Day of the Law   The Buddha-way of Sowing

In the *"Selection of Time"* we are advised: *"One who wishes to study the teachings of the Buddha must FIRST learn to understand the time."* ND, MS Vol. 3 - p.79

The historical Buddha, *Shakyamuni* appeared some 2,500 to 3,000 years ago and his oral teachings became known as the 84,000 teachings, or the faith to answer all questions. The Former and Middle Day of the Law lasted until around 1,100 c.e.

In the *Daijuku Sutra* we learn: *"the first five hundred years after the Buddha's passing will be the Age of enlightenment, and the next five hundred years, the age of meditation. The next five hundred years will be an age of reading, reciting and listening, and the next five hundred years, the age of building temples and stupas."* The *Lotus Sutra* states that in the fifth five hundred years there will be an age opening the door to the Buddha-way of Sowing once again. If we accept that the *Shakyamuni* was born over 2,500 years ago, then the Latter Day of the Law began around 1,100 b.c.e. From a farmer's stand point it may seem backwards that you have the Harvest before the Maturing and Sowing. This is explained as follows: the Buddha left behind an Age of Enlightenment which is gradually lost, then comes a new age of Learning and Realization and then again an age of Sowing in the ever turning eternal Buddha Dharma Wheel.

"Many are the spiritual pathways that eventually lead One to the main Free-Way"

The correct selection of the time is not limited to faith; right timing is vital to so many things in life and nature. From a Buddhist perspective the concept of "time" is determined according to the fusion of One's *spiritual capacity*. As humans we do not have the ability to penetrate the three existence's of past, present and future, but we can understand whether the timing is right in this life for our spiritual development. The Buddhist philosophy works towards harmony and peace within, thorough action, compassion and spiritual sustain-ability. How wonderful and profound that You are discovering Your Buddha nature at this time.

Worthy of Respect

Let's consider some reasons why the Buddha Dharma is such a beautiful concept and worthy of One's respect:

1] *Shakyamuni* Buddha lived a long, healthy and happy lifetime, living for eighty years on earth. He was born a prince, his father was head of a state, not unlike a modern day Premier, or State Governor. He was surrounded by wealth and family, he married and had a son. In his early twenties we are told he couldn't accept that only the very, very few should have all the wealth and power, while the masses struggled with poverty, sickness, old age and death. He left his wife and son in the care of his father to go off into the mountains to find the truth of life. After six years of heavy abstinence he realized that this was not the correct way to live either and came back to live a more normal lifestyle. Shortly thereafter, he realized the ultimate Way of Life, which became known as the *Middle Pathway.* Re-joined with his father, wife and son [his mother died shortly after his birth] he travelled India extensively, gathering followers. Over fifty years he taught through various methods *the living philosophy of life* which became known as the 84,000 teachings. From the ancient Sanskrit language we learn that "buddha" translates as **"awakened or enlightened."** This Buddha was human.

2] *The Buddha-way is One with the* eternal, infinite, universal Law, encompassing all nature, life and death. A Buddhist believes that each individual is responsible for his or her life and destiny in the past, present and future.

3] By the time *Shakyamuni* returned to universal Nirvana, much of the country of India had literally converted to his gracious teachings, putting aside cast and inequalities as both the Brahma Priesthood and early Hindu spiritual practices were temporarily left behind as partial truths. At his death when he was asked who was to be the leader after he passed on, he said, *"what have I been teaching all these years, but that you must follow no man, rather follow the eternal Universal Law."* He did not say follow my teachings even, he said; learn and realize the Universal Law

and *follow what is right for You.* The Buddhist philosophy teaches that all life eventually flows to Enlightenment.

Understanding the Teachings

When it comes to our Spiritual Health then, how can we judge what is right for us ?

Perhaps the following can act as a guideline:

1] The teacher, or messenger should be enlightened to all that is past, present, future

2] The teaching or doctrine should be without error and based on the principle of Cause and Effect through documentary evidence of the teaching.

3] The belief should be rational and capable of being believed by all people

4] The rules for practice should be universal and non controlling

5] The benefit of belief throughout the practice and study should be suited to a teaching which is not superficial and temporary, but all encompassing and eternal.

The Buddha-way teaches the entity of all phenomena and reaches beyond to other worlds while offering deep insight of human life in the here and NOW.

Three Proofs

The Buddha Way is based on three Proofs: Documentary, Theoretical and Actual. With regards to the three proofs *Nichiren* states: "actual proof surpasses both documentary and theoretical." In other words whatever faith, religion or spiritual pathway we choose it must have *actual proof* in our daily life. I hope you will come to see that the teaching allows personal freedom, happiness and a peaceful inner strength not based on a mythical world apart from our human world. *Documentary* proof is used to determine whether the teaching is supported by the teachings of the founder. *Theoretical* proof is to ascertain that the teaching is based on the concept of Cause and Effect. *Actual* proof is proof that your "conscious communication" with the *Eternal Law* is not just theoretical but has *real proof* in your daily life.

At the end of these Sharing Sessions my hope is that You will have a new and deep understanding of the Buddha-way, that you may desire to make it an active part of your faith and wisdom HL

Introduction To Faith Practice and Study

Faith

Buddhists believe in a higher power, the Universal Law of Cause and Effect, the power of the universe that is eternal and ever changing. Worldwide it is estimated that there are 2.1 billion Christians, 600 million Buddhists, 1.8 billion Muslims, 900 million Hindu, 1.1 billion none believers and a variety of other spiritual practices. Peaceful harmony as a goal is a long way off as too much of the world believes God is either on their side, or they don't believe at all. Peace through faith is a long way off but spiritual awareness is growing.

Faith, practice and study is the Threefold Treasure that allows an individual to attain levels of learning, realization, and wisdom; this leads One to enlightenment. Buddhists carry out daily practice in order to call forth *Right Thought, Right Motivation* and *Right Action* in life.

People take faith for many reasons. Sometimes it is due to what we are taught at the footsteps of parents, sometimes it is because we disapprove of our parents beliefs, sometimes it is out of hope, sometimes it is out of despair and sometimes because we have seen a positive change in a friend. There are many reasons One takes faith, yet as we have seen over a billion humans have no faith at all.

Buddhists take faith to call forth their Buddha nature, to overcome One's Karma, to help face life's challenges, and to defeat mental illusion. They seek the wisdom to understand the difference between those things in life that they can control and those that they cannot. Faith means different things to different people. For some it is a *Specific* making of daily offerings with an understanding that faith is a fusion of communication with all that is. While for others it is only a matter of bumper stickers, or praying in times of need or crisis. *Nichiren* a compassionate

Buddha in our *Latter Day of the Law* states: "to have faith is the basis of the Buddha Dharma" ND

From statements like this we can quickly realize that Buddhists are no different than others when it comes to understanding the doctrine. Faith is a *master key* that can unlock the doors of ignorance and illusion. The teachings can open the door, but One must walk through. The Buddha's teachings tell us we must have pure and simple faith if we are to find awareness, bliss, wisdom and enlightenment as we are. The goal of faith, practice and study is absolute freedom and an understanding of life and death. Therefore, one needs to understand that *blind faith* or faith because someone else tells us to have faith is not the way to truth or wisdom.

Practice

You can be self taught, enter the World of Learning by the reading of books and materials by others in order to become knowledgeable about a subject such as the Buddha Dharma. The first practice is through self action. It makes sense to understand without practice, faith would mean very little, like some distant hope. From the *Mahayana* Buddhist school of philosophy we come to understand that faith in Oneself is only the first manner of practice and does not lead to full wisdom or enlightenment. Through study of the Buddhist Dharma one realizes the need to utilize faith, practice and study not only for Oneself, but also in a commitment to the living and the dead that peace through full enlightenment may be attained.

The second method of practice then means, having attained a level of personal unity within Oneself, One becomes happy to share the joy and wisdom with others, understanding that everyone is empowered to make a difference for peaceful means. Again from *Nichiren*, "without practice and study, there can be no Buddhist-way." Here we clearly are told that blind faith leads only to a very narrow pathway. Practice consists of personal growth for Oneself and for the sake of others. Practice for oneself means physical, mental and spiritual development in a consistent, disciplined manner.

Study

In today's world, the *Internet* opens the door to endless research and data. From a Buddhist perspective this is what is known as the *World of Learning*, the *Sixth World* of the *Ten Dharma Worlds* in Buddhist philosophy. Through learning we are expressing our seeking spirit in a natural manner of discovery. At all times when seeking development of our Health, physical, mental, spiritual, it is important to research throughly that we may know what is right for our personal well being. There is so much misinformation and false information in the world of Learning that it is important to protect Oneself by asking for assistance in *Realizing* what is true for Oneself.

Having attained a level of faith, it is important to try through practice that which we have learned. Without practice we soon become busy with other things and our spiritual health goes into limbo. No one can make progress in life or establish what is right for them without effort. Therefore, the compassion of the Buddha explains *"exert yourself in the two ways of practice and study"* ND The Buddha Dharma teaches that when our Buddha nature manifests from within our lives, it will obtain protection from the universal *Shoten Zenjin,* messengers or energy forces of the Infinite Law. Practice brings protection to our environment and our personal aura. Life's challenges become easier to understand and take lessons from.

This is one of the fundamental principles of the Buddhist philosophy! In considering the growth of our *spiritual health* we can understand that both practice and study arise from our seeking spirit and a deep appreciation of gratitude for the blessings we receive whether we see them or not. Every human is very unique and special. Every human has a story to tell. The Lotus Sutra says: *I deeply respect You,* The Nirvana Sutra says: *"All living things possess the Buddha nature"*

Faith takes conviction, but the rewards are indeed great. When we carry out practice and study as expressions of our faith, actual proof appears, which in turn leads to an active lifestyle of living in the higher Worlds of Joy, health and happiness at all times. By practicing One's Buddha nature false desires, mental illusions and negative karma will be replaced by deep understanding and the higher *World of Realization.* How wonderful !

Is Buddha A God? Is God A Buddha?

Before considering the concepts of God or Buddha, let's consider what it means to be human. Faith is a personal journey, Your spiritual Health is dependent on your choices, your beliefs. One universal characteristic of human life is its uncertainty. The most promising career could fail unexpectedly, and today's commitment to love another forever often ends much sooner than that. Good health, can turn to sickness, wealth may come and go; in short the human condition is one of limitations and temporary existence.

The role of faith is to enable human beings to transcend the uncertainty of their finite state by believing in a more eternal principle. In the Judaeo-Christian, Hindu and Muslim traditions this eternal unchanging truth has been personified as God, the creator and ruler of the Universe. So, where does the concept of god come from? Originally there where a multitude of pagan gods. The god of Light, a god to *invoke,* rain for the crops, the defeat of armies, the god of Zeus, the Greek *Theos* and the Latin *Deus*. Out of respect and fear for many centuries the name *God* could not be spoken. Signs and sounds were first used, human and animal sacrifices made. Eventually Uhwa, Jehovah, Allah and God became the spoken word.

Buddhists view this eternal unchanging truth as an impersonal *eternal, universal Law* of Cause and Effect that permeates all life and the universe itself. This Law is best described in the Buddha's highest teaching contained in the **Lotus Sutra,** or wisdom teachings, the Buddhist bible if you will. Contained in the Book, this Law is defined to encompass all the qualities usually associated with God, such as infinite wisdom, boundless compassion and eternity. It goes further through natural law and explains the entity of all Phenomena.

Most religious teachings in the western tradition hold that humans and god are of a differing nature, humans can never become God. The Buddha-way teaches that the Law is One's life itself, the true entity of all phenomena. Everything is connected,

One is all, all is one! In other words either god is everything, I.e: a part of man, woman, plant, tree, rock, water, fire, good, bad, love, hate, fear, kindness, meanness, war or god is not. Nothing separates human beings from this truth. All is One. According to the Buddha Dharma people suffer in this world because they are unaware of this wonderful whole truth, everything is of the same phenomenal nature and nothing exists by itself.

The Buddha Dharma teaches that life is not about will power, control, supplication to a God, causing war in the name of God, etc. Life is about taking responsibility discovering the truth "within" tapping an inner source happiness, strength and wisdom. In this way the Buddha sets the individual free from dependence on some superior being outside him or her self enabling the discovery of ones highest nature and freedom from suffering. As we noted, the word "Buddha" comes from the Sanskrit word meaning "to awaken." A Buddha is not a god or an innately superior being. Millions of buddhas live in all ten directions, in our universe and the many other universes beyond our cosmos. A Buddha is One who has awakened to the eternal universal Law within the reality of life, beyond life and death. The Buddha Dharma makes no claim to divine revelation, but rather revelation of the Way, Light and Truth of All phenomena. From a Buddhist perspective the eternal life-force or god, is a natural part of all phenomena. The historical Buddha *Shakyamuni* or Siddhartha, *Gautama*, lived on earth some 2,600 to 3,000 years ago in the Former Day of the Law. We find the following in the sixteenth Chapter of the **Lotus Sutra:** *"the time which has passed since I attained Buddhahood passes one hundred, thousand, ten thousand, hundred thousand, nayuta, asogi other worlds. I made my appearance, teaching in many different worlds, using different names. All this I did through different methods of teaching that were suited to the capacity of the people."*

The Magic Mystery Tour

Throughout time, stories and parables have been a way to explain to the masses the various meanings of life and death. The Buddhist philosophy incorporates all that came before its teachings some

3,000 years ago and merges it with today. The Buddha Dharma is always about NOW and the magic mystery tour we are on as humans. Included in the teachings are many lesson stories such as .. BRAHMA a god said to live in the first of the four meditation heavens in the world of form above Mount Summeru ruler of the *Saha* world of endurance. In Indian mythology he was regarded as the personification of the fundamental universal principle. He was adopted as one of the two major tutelary gods. INDRA the other major tutelary god, was one of the twelve gods said to protect the world in all directions. Originally the god of Thunder in Indian mythology. He was later incorporated into Buddhist teachings as a protective deity. He is said to live in a palace called *Correct Views* in the Trayastrimsha Heaven. Served by Four Heavenly Kings, he governs the other thirty two gods of that heaven.

The Buddha's of the Ten Directions come from natures directions, symbolically, Zenith, or upper Heavens, North, element of air, South, element of oceans, East, element of humanity, West, element of water, Northwest, element of wind, Southeast, element of fire, Northeast, element of earth, Southwest, element of negative energy, along with the energies of the Sun, Moon and Stars, and the Nadir or downward Heavens. We can see how much easier it might be to simply believe in a God.

On the **GOHONZON** Mandala, inscribed by *Nichiren Daishonin* the protector of the East, *Jikokuten,* is located on the upper right as one faces it, *Komokuten,* the protector of the West, on the lower right, *Bishamonten,* the protector of the North, on the upper left, and *Zojoten*, the protector of the South, on the lower left. As for the connection between these stories, the Buddha of our Latter Day of the Law, Nichiren explains the relationship between a Buddha and an ordinary person: *"While deluded, one is called a common mortal, but once enlightened, a Buddha. Even a tarnished mirror will shine like a jewel if it is polished. A mind which presently is clouded by illusions originating from the innate darkness of life is like a tarnished mirror, but once it is polished it will become clear, reflecting the enlightenment of immutable truth. Arouse deep faith and polish your mirror night and day."* Nichiren Daishonin, On Attaining Buddhahood

Enlightenment

"Though a cave may be in total darkness for a million years the moment we bring a light inside, the cave must receive the light and become illuminated." Through faith you will ignite the flame of light and happiness in your life but you ask, what is enlightenment?

> *"Enlightenment is the highest quality of the mind; it is free from all [the limiting] attributes of subjectivity. It is like unto space penetrating everywhere, within the unity of all"*
> Asvaghosa, The Awakening of Faith

Here then is how we attain enlightenment as common mortals or just as one is. The *Lotus Sutra* shares that one can attain Buddhahood in this lifetime in One's present form as a common mortal. The concept of attaining enlightenment in one's present form contrasts with that of the attainment through transformation over a period of countless lifetimes. This is a big difference between provisional Buddhist teachings and the teachings of the Mahayana essential Buddhist philosophy.

We are working towards enlightenment when we are in the *World of Learning* as we study facts and knowledge, as the truth is revealed to us, as we become free from fear, ignorance, prejudice and false views. We are receiving enlightenment when we are in the *World of Realization* as we perceive truth without having to be told or taught but JUST KNOW. We are *enlightened* at those moments when we are overtaken by the great life force of *bliss and joy beyond words !* Nichiren again tells us, that earthly desires are enlightenment. "When one chants *Namu Myoho Renge Kyo* even during sexual union of man and woman, then earthly desires are enlightenment and the sufferings of life and death are nirvana. Whereas sufferings are nirvana only when one realizes that the entity of human life throughout its cycle of birth and death is neither born nor destroyed." ND

Insentient Phenomena

What about plants, animals and trees, or anything else which has neither emotion nor consciousness can they receive enlightenment? This is called the *enlightenment of insentient beings*. The principal that insentient beings can attain Buddhahood derives from *T'ien Tai Chi I's* doctrine of component principles in the *Realm of the Environment*, that is, that a living being and its nonliving environment, or sentient and insentient beings, both manifest the same true entity of life and both therefore have the same potential for Buddhahood. The ancient scholar *Miao-lo* tells us, "a plant, a tree, a pebble, a speck of dust -- each has the innate Buddha nature, along with the other causes and conditions needed to attain Buddhahood". (Kongobei Ron) All is One, and All can become enlightened.

We must not seek enlightenment outside ourselves. Our study of Buddha Dharma will not relieve us of sufferings until we can begin to perceive the essence of our true self. *Tien Tai Chi I* states, "If one does not perceive the essence of his own life, his past heavy sins cannot be blotted out". In other words, in order to attain enlightenment we must accept that daily problems in life, large and small appear in this lifetime for our Benefit, allowing us to *expiate our karma* and grow through our courage, faith and accomplishments. The Infinite Law teaches us of the law of Cause and Effect, for every action there is an equal reaction; this too is the law of physics. So we must come to use *Right Thought*, have *Right Motivation* in order to take *Right Action* in our dealings with all things, places, and people in order to attain enlightenment.

Through the courage to accept our character defects, and our life's challenges, we can make a difference. We can learn through faith, practice and study to change our *"poison into medicine."* It is through our individual *"human revolution"* that like other Buddha's, we, too can attain enlightenment; not in some distant heaven or universe but right here in the pure land of earth, in the Time of Here and NOW. Our personal self is a thing of the moment, being born, being sick from time to time, becoming elderly and dying; but the real self, through the power of *"Myo"* [eternal wonder] is eternal. As we live this life, in faith, practice and study, we can harmoniously unify and reach for enlightenment.

Through Faith, Practice and Study, we take on the condition of wisdom, filled with vitality, as we grow in empathy, compassion, love, and patience we are being enlightened! As we find our self at peace, living in today we will find moments of blissful enlightenment. Now we have an understanding of our ability to attain enlightenment. How fortunate we are!

"Enlightenment is not an eternal or transcendental state, as many might assume. Rather it is a condition of the highest wisdom, vitality and good fortune wherein the individual can shape his or her destiny, find fulfilment in daily activities, and come to understand his or her purpose in being alive" ND

Summary of First Sharing Session

The eternal, universal Law that is the Buddha-way is ever changing and eternal.

Within the Buddha Dharma Wheel of wisdom there are Three major time periods:

The Buddha Way of the Harvest, the Former Day of the Law, 1,000 years

The Buddha Way of Maturing, the Middle Day of the Law, 1,000 years

The Buddha Way of Sowing, our Latter Day of the Law. 10,000 years

We have learned that there are many, Buddha's throughout time and space. That *Gautama Shakyamuni* Buddha, the historical earthly Buddha, appeared on earth approximately three thousand years ago.

We heard of *Taho* Buddha who came from a far Eastern universe in support of *Shakyamuni* while he was teaching the *Lotus Sutra;* a teaching that lays out the story of the universal way of all phenomena, and the fusion between humans and the natural, infinite, eternal, Law. We explored the information that near the beginning of the Latter Day of the Law, a fisherman's son from Japan, the Great Sage, *Nichiren Daishonin* appeared and after many years of study made claim that the Buddhists of his day were no longer following a faithful pathway but had let politics, power and desire get in the way of correct practice. He founded the *Mahayana Nichiren Buddhist Sect*, as a way for all people to practice the Buddha's Law in the time of NOW, the Latter Day of the Law.

We shared that from the Buddhist perspective god is simply All natural phenomena in our universal environment and that humans naturally seek more than the wonders of this lifetime as part of the wholeness of all existence of past, present and future.

We shared, that like all philosophies, it was first the oral story telling that made up the Way of understanding. We agreed that there should be *Three Proofs* in discussing any faith, practice or study. It should be good for us, actual proof. It should be supported by documentary and theoretical proof. And, the proof that is most important should be *"actual proof."* Spiritual freedom, happiness and a peaceful inner strength should be based on faith, practice, study, and actual proof in our daily lives.

"Do You Believe Your Meditations are Heard, Or are You just here for the Muffins" HL

Discovering Your Buddha Nature

The Buddha - The Law - The Beings

Sharing Session   Two of Seven

1] The Law of Cause & Effect
2] Belief In the Mahayana *Nichiren* School
3] Needs Answered ~ Personal Meditation & Prayer
4] Precepts of the Latter Day of the Law
5] Fusion of The Person & The Law
6] Oneness Realization ~ Actuality of the Buddha-way

Cause and Effect ~ *The Universal Factor*

All phenomena are subject to the strict law of cause and effect, the results of karma or action both in living and inanimate life. Consequently, the state of an individual's present life, his or her destiny, is the summation of all previous causes. It is no exaggeration to say that this principle of cause and effect is at the foundation of all religions, philosophies and sciences, and has nothing to do with being born a sinner. This doctrine is summarized in the Buddhist theory known as **Ichinen Sanzen.** Which is an understanding of how the universe works, which we will study later on.

In the *Middle Day of the Law* the great Teacher, Scholar/Priest from China, *T'ien-Tai Chih-I* formulated the ten major schools of Buddhist teachings and classified them into five periods and eight major teachings according to their chronological order, content and method of teaching. Over his lifetime he came to realize and believe through the study of all the scriptures of the various teachings that the highest philosophy of Buddha Dharma was to be found in the Scripture of the Lotus Blossom of the Fine Dharma. Within the Lotus Sutra he found the principle of *Ichinen Sanzen*, with an explanation of The Ten Factors and The Three Realms of Existence. Even though life is eternal, it is contained within the momentary existence of this lifetime. In other words, the present invariably becomes the past, and the future quickly becomes the present. Accordingly, each moment is an actual existence characterized by the concept of a void or *Ku*, in which presence is in itself nothingness and nothingness is in itself presence. The moment is quite simply, NOW!

There is no existence outside this moment, eternity is but a series of these NOW moments. Therefore, at times we experience happiness, at other times we cry out of sadness, and at still other times we feel discouraged and disappointed – all as a result of our *Karmic* causes of the past that are manifested in our present life.

In order to firmly establish a life condition of enlightenment in the present and future, we must realize that our present attitude and conduct are the key elements that will determine our happiness or misfortune. It is of foremost importance to be confident that it is possible for you to construct an eternally indestructible life condition of health, happiness and wisdom. Wherever there is water, the moon will be reflected in it. In the same way when we understand *the Law of Cause and Effect*, then the Buddha will reside without fail in our lives. A *master key* to enlightenment in the here and now is to attain No Doubt.

Based upon our thoughts, words, and deeds in the present moment, the Law of Cause and Effect will positively or negatively shape our future. Failure to recognize this fact leads us to unhappiness, while wisdom from faith, practice and study enables us to cut the life cycle of various sufferings. When we think that the roles we play in each other's lives are based on chance and limited to the present lifetime alone, we live very shallow lives. When we study our ego and search for true self, we are making the cause to attract enriching relationships based on our own higher life condition. As humans, we have contact and interaction with people on a daily basis. As insignificant as our relations sometimes seem, an Attitude for better or worse can profoundly affect another person's life, and the life of others, in time reflecting on our community, our country and the world. Therefore we should always seek out environments which have a good influence on us. The Buddha-way is a practical manner of faith, practice and study.

Eternal Teachings

We all hope and meditate on various matters because of differences in our current circumstances and background. It is important to understand that the fundamental source of these differences is our individual karma. Chanting, meditation and prayer help us to transfer negative karma into positive karma, from suffering into health and happiness. *"If you want to understand the causes that existed in the past, look at the results as they are manifested in the present. If you want to understand what results will be manifested in the future, look at the causes that exist in the present."* Nichiren Daishonin - 1257 c.e.

"In the fifth five hundred years, the eternal teachings shall spread and benefit human kind far into the future." Tien Tai Chi'I - [538-597]   This is accomplished through faith, practice and study. To those who receive the Precepts and take the vows of specific practice, the *Nichiren* Buddha Sangha or members, make offerings of five daily prayers. It is said that if One can master the meanings of these profound prayers, One can master the teachings of the Buddha.

Belief In the Mahayana Nichiren School

Meditating twice daily with Five Prayers of specific devotion *Nichiren* Buddhists give thanks for the manifestation of the **Gohonzon** Mandala, an object worthy of deep respect for our present age, the Buddha Time of Sowing. Now, we will reflect on specific Meditation of the Second and Fourth prayers of the Essential teachings of the *Nichiren* Mahayana tradition.

This practice embodies the principle of connecting the *Three Treasures* of the infinite, eternal Law, the Buddha and the Beings. One sincerely expresses respect to the universal Law, to the Buddha, to the teachings of the Buddha and the Essential *Honmon* teachings contained in the *Lotus Sutra*. Buddhists believe in the fusion of Objective reality *Kyo* and Subjective wisdom *Chi*, and the fusion of the Oneness of the Person and the Law. Buddhists believe in the entity of eternity without beginning or ending known as *Kuon Ganjo*. Mahayana Buddhists understand the workings of our universe through Ten Factors and the eternal coexistence of Ten Worlds through the true entity of all phenomena, known as *Ichinen Sanzen*. Buddhists believe in the Way of absolute freedom.

Ten Articles of Faith

1] Manifestation of the object worthy of great respect the *Gohonzon* mandala

2] *Three Treasures*, the Law, the Buddha and the Beings [Sangha & Priesthood]

3] Oneness of the Buddhist Law ~ *Infinite Eternal Universal Law*

4] *Lotus Sutra* and the Essential Teachings ~ *Honmon*

5] Fusion of Objective reality *Kyo* and Subjective wisdom *Chi*

6] Fusion of Oneness of the Person and the Law, One's connection to eternal life

7] Entity of eternity without beginning or ending ~ *Kuon Ganjo*

8] Universal Oneness of All phenomena ~ *Ichinen Sanzen*

9] Eternal coexistence of the *Ten Worlds* within the *Ten Factors*

10] Buddha of absolute freedom

1] One who is Karmically fortunate may in this lifetime discover the *Gohonzon Mandala*, of the *Nichiren* Buddha School. It is the respected, worthy, mandala of meditation, visualization and Oneness of the Buddha's teachings. It is a wooden and paper scroll, the object worthy of deep profound respect in which all the precepts of the essential teachings are written in black sumi ink. The messages outlined on the *Gohonzon* are profound, exciting and deep, containing various aspects of the Buddha Dharma. It is a scroll of profound significance!

2] *"Those who visit this place can instantly expiate the sins they have committed since the infinite past and transform their illusions into wisdom, their errors into truth and their sufferings into freedom."* ND   When we understand the validity of the Three Treasures we make this possible. There are variations on the interpretation of the Three Treasures. For example, there are various Buddhas such as: *Shakyamuni* the historical earthly Buddha; *Amida* a future distant universe or Pure Land Buddha, *Dainichi* a Buddha of the esoteric teachings; and *Nichiren* in our Latter Day of the Law. The *Priesthood* is a third Treasure, while others see the *Sangha* or Buddhist members as the third Treasure. When we include the Three Treasures as the Buddha, the Law and the Beings, everyone and everything is included in our Latter Day of the Law.

Nichiren states in the Niike Gosho: *"If one truly understands Buddha Dharma he/she should show this in his/her respect for the Priesthood, reverence for the Law and offerings to the Buddha."* The Three Treasures are further defined as ultimately being One entity. While the Treasure of the Law is eternal *Kuon Ganjo* an immutable Original Law of the simultaneity of *Cause and Effect* that spans the three existences of past, present and future. This Law is revealed due to the existence of humans who have the potential to be enlightened to the infinite, universal Law. Therefore, it is not possible to separate the Law, the Buddha and the Beings.

3] The Infinite, Eternal, Universal Law: *"Through some deeply eternal causal life chain, we have found the teaching that enables*

one to awaken to the eternity of one's personal life force and establish an inner joy transcending birth and death." The eternal Law always was and always will be. Through the Law one comes to see one's Buddha nature and enlightenment in ones personal daily life. As we come to realize this, a desire grows within us to let other people share in this benefit. As we come to realize that our purpose on earth is to find peace within and then to share it with others, our attitude and motivation towards life and those we share life with changes from the schooled competitive edge to spiritual sustain-ability. The important point to realize is that the *Infinite Eternal Universal Law* has always come before the need for a god, mythical saviour or deity.

4] The *Lotus Sutra* and the essential teaching *Honmon* , was one of the Buddha's final teachings and was taught over a period of the last eight years of his life. In the Lotus Sutra he explains that his purpose is to free all people from suffering and for them to understand their personal potential for deep wisdom and Enlightenment in this lifetime. In the second chapter of the Lotus Sutra, he explains that no phenomenon is in any way different from the true entity of life, that is, the ultimate truth. All things in the universe are one and the same. They are manifestations of this truth. Permeating the cycle of birth and death and all other transient phenomena, there exists an eternal and unchanging truth, or entity of life. By becoming enlightened to it, one can overcome his/her sufferings in this endurance world. The Lotus Sutra or *Myoho~Renge~ Kyo*, reveals that the universe and the individual self are one and the same. Our life is, itself, a particle of the macrocosm. *Myo* is the power given to the eternal nature of life, and *ho* to its manifestations. *Renge*, the lotus flower, symbolizes the simultaneous nature of Cause and Effect, the wonder of this Law.

Once we realize that our own life is contained within the Eternal Law, we will realize that so are the lives of all others. *Kyo* or sound manifestation, is the manner in which we are able to share this wonderful Law. When we say the *Lotus Sutra* we mean all the eight books and all the twenty eight chapters contained therein. In the same way when we say the word Canadian, European or

Asian, we mean all the people from all cultures, faiths, careers, and economic backgrounds. The Lotus Sutra, by reaching back into antiquity, teaches its message for today. And, *Nichiren Daishonin* explains how we accomplish this now in our *Latter Day of the Law*. So when we say the *Lotus Sutra*, we mean the entity of the Law, the Buddha and the Beings.

5] The Fusion of Subject *Kyo* and Object *Chi:* the Buddha Dharma defines enlightenment as the fusion of these two: the *objective reality* of One's Buddha nature and the *subjective wisdom* to realize it. That is the objective reality inherent within one's life and the subjective wisdom to realize that truth for oneself. "To see the Buddha nature within one's self." In the *Lotus Sutra* there is a great ceremony in the air as a method of teaching the people through story telling. *Taho* Buddha, seated in the Treasure Tower, represents objective reality, *Shakyamuni* Buddha represents subjective wisdom. Sitting together in the Tower they represent the fusion of reality and wisdom. From the viewpoint of the living philosophy of the Buddha Dharma, *Taho* Buddha is *the Buddha nature inherent in our personal lives. Shakyamuni* Buddha represents the *wisdom to realize our Buddha nature.* Through faith, practice and study we come to an inner realization of the potential for an enlightened existence on earth, right here and right now. Through our subjective wisdom we become completely fused with the objective reality of Life and Death as One. The Buddha Dharma defines *Enlightenment* as this fusion of subject and object, the wisdom to realize this truth in our life. Through Meditation we come to realize that the Body, the Mind and the Spirit are One. A suggestion from the *Nirvana* Sutra is to understand that *"one should become the master of his mind rather than letting his mind master him/her."* In *Nichiren* Buddhist practice this is accomplished with the daily performance of "sound meditation" or chanting called *Daimoku* and through the meaning of the Five Prayers. In this Sharing Session we are looking at the Second and Fourth prayerful meditations.

6] One of the factors contained in the fusion of the *Oneness of the Person and the Law* is wisdom. So, from a Buddhist point of view what is wisdom? There are several characteristics, but

let's consider it here as the capacity to see Oneself objectively, to see One's "true-self" or "Spiritual nature." To relate this to the emotion of Love, it corresponds to a clear recognition of what attitude One has taken and is taking in relationship to both the people in our life and to the nature of life on earth. The co-relationship of the *Ten Worlds* plays a great part in our ability to perceive our true nature, based on up bringing, education, and in our process of personality formation.

7] ***Kuon Ganjo*** translates into eternity, without beginning or ending, allowing one to eternally inherit the three enlightened properties of life: Health, Happiness and Contentment. We are of the Oneness of all life and death, without beginning or ending. Here is a deep Meditation for us!

8 & 9] A major doctrine of understanding the living philosophy of the Buddha Dharma comes from the concept of ***Ichinen Sanzen***. This spiritual and scientific understanding of the infinite Law as defined in the Lotus Sutra over 2,600 years ago, was developed in the *Middle Day of the Law* by the Teacher, Scholar/Priest *Tien Tai Chi'I*. With this knowledge one comes to understand why some are born financially rich and some poor, why some have good health and others die too young. It allows us to confront all human sufferings alike and to have a complete understanding of our environment. *Ichinen Sanzen* was developed from the Second Roll of the ***Lotus Sutra,*** where the *Ten Factors* are pronounced. Deep within all that lives and dies is the eternal and unchanging Law or entity of life which transcends both birth and death. This philosophy of the *Mutual Possession* of the Ten Worlds and Ten Factors, the possibility of Three Thousand Realms in a momentary existence of life is known as *Ichinen Sanzen*. We will be sharing more on this concept of the Buddha-way in another Sharing Session.

10] The Buddha of absolute freedom is Joy itself. It is an understanding that we are not bound by our *Karma*. One is free to attain enlightenment through personal growth in this lifetime. Our freedom is being shaped by our daily actions. We are responsible for our self and for helping others attain this freedom. We can do this by assisting other humans discover their Buddha nature.

"A Buddhist is One who by becoming enlightened to the Oneness of all phenomena acquires indestructible happiness and peace." HL

Personal Meditation Needs Answered ~
Personal Prayer

In explaining prayer as part of ones life-force, *Nichiren Daishonin* explains that faith is vital and that with faith comes all life's answers for both now and future existence. ND The *Nirvana Sutra* says: *"What Buddha's take as their teacher is the Law. Therefore, the Buddhas honor, respect and make offerings to it."* In the *Hoben* Chapter or Second Book of the *Lotus Sutra* we find *"[visitors] come from ten thousands of millions of lands."* Indeed this must be a good place to pray, find enlightenment and know that our meditations and prayers must be heard.

We are told of the power of prayer again in the following: *"we know that the prayers offered by a practitioner of the Lotus Sutra will be answered just as an echo answers a sound, as a shadow follows a form, as the reflection of the moon appears in clear water, as a mirror collects dewdrops, as lodestone attracts iron, as amber attracts particles of dust, or as a bright mirror reflects the color of an object."* ND

Through our meditation and prayer, we are able to think clear thoughts opening up the trinity of body-mind-spirit, producing positive karma. Buddhist prayer is a journey towards freedom, but ones prayers should be based on inner actuality not blind faith. When we understand the where and why of the doctrine, then the theology behind the doctrine can be acknowledged. Through One's power of prayer much can be accomplished as the *Shoten Zenjin*, messengers and guardians, sources of energy and light, are increasingly nourished by our conscious communication, so that their life-force can send forth protection from within the Oneness of the infinite, eternal universal Law.

It is through One's personal powers, prayers and meditations that we make sure our motivations are trustworthy, that the energy forces of the universe accepting, feeling our offerings will be able to provide a beneficial effect. It is in the *Fourth* daily prayer that we specifically ask: "for the attainment of peace within, peace for our community, and the Buddhist concept of *Kosen Rufu*. Peace without borders, inclusive to All people and cultures, spiritual sustain-ability within the Buddha dharma.

We meditate to expiate our negative karma, daily purify our faith and practice, asking for our needs and making offerings for our friends and family, so that we may attain enlightenment in this and all future existence. Our empowerment is great when combined with a wise and enlightened earthly desire.

The Buddha's Words

In the *Mahayana Nichiren* tradition, there are two methods of meditation and prayer, they are known as the Primary practice and the Supplementary practice. During morning and evening meditations called *Gongyo*, one may recite the prose sections of the *Expedient Devices*, Second Chapter and the *Life Span*, Sixteenth Chapter of the *Lotus Sutra*.

The primary practice is the Five~In~One, sound meditation, chanting of the all inclusive title of the Buddha's highest teachings as contained within the Lotus Sutra. Chanting **Nam~Myoho~Renge ~Kyo**, is called the *primary* practice. While recitation of the *Expedient Devices* and the *Life Span* portions of the *Lotus* teachings, the words of the Buddha in the classic Chinese ancient language, is called the *supplementary* practice. The merit one gains from the discipline of consistently practicing this way is powerful and immeasurable. The fortune one accumulates is often inconspicuous.

Fundamental Means & Eternal Life Chapters of Lotus Sutra

So why out of all the chapters of the *Lotus Sutra,* do Buddhists recite these particular portions? *Nichiren* indicates the reason in the 'Recitation of the *Hoben* [Expedient Devices] and *Juryo* [Eternal Life] Chapters', "(Even) though none of the chapters of the Lotus Sutra is negligible, out of all the twenty-eight chapters,

35

the *Hoben* and *Juryo* chapters are particularly superior and praise worthy. The remaining chapters are all like the branches and leaves [of these two chapters]. Therefore, for your regular practice you should learn and recite the prose sections of the *Hoben* and *Juryo* chapters." Shinpen, p 303; Ref: MW., Vol. 6, p.10

The *Hoben* chapter is the core of the Theoretical teachings of the Lotus Sutra, and the *Juryo* chapter is the core of the Essential teachings. *Nichiren Daishonin* began the practice of reciting these chapters daily. For over 750 years *Nichiren* Buddhists have chanted and prayed these prayers daily for world peace and spiritual sustain-ability. At the Head Temple in Japan, the chanting of *Nam~Myoho~Renge~Kyo* goes on twenty four hours of everyday in a Temple dedicated to *Kosen Rufu,* the growth of the Buddha-way, and worldwide compassion.

Thus, the recitation of the Sutra functions to augment the merit of our meditation, while chanting the Daimoku of *Nam~Myoho~Renge~Kyo* is the primary practice. As we chant and follow the precepts of the *Lotus Sutra,* our empowerment cannot be denied due to the law of *Cause and Effect.* Sound Meditation and prayer are part of Ones faith, practice and study. How wonderful!

Power of Meditation & Prayer

Approach the universal Law knowing that All is One.
Feel Your Buddha nature within You reaching out.

Know that *Your Enlightenment* is in progress,
Your meditations and prayers heard and affected.
Feel the fusion and vibration of the moment.

In daily practice the most important
significance of Meditation and Prayer
is to be found *"within"* your Buddha nature.

As one offers sincere meditation and prayer
an empowerment is felt and acted upon
"within" the universal Law of Cause & Effect.

From Power, Prayers & Meditations, Henry Landry

Precepts of the Latter Day of the Law

Everyday Buddhist practice consists of an active offering within the three types of Learning known as *Precepts, Meditation* and *Wisdom. Precepts:* refers to the principle of preventing injustice through action by leading a life of example through the three categories of mental, verbal and physical deeds. This is the precept of leading an active, dynamic, healthy, life; preventing injustice through meditation and wisdom.

Meditation: "Chanting ~ sound meditation" and *"Kan'nen* ~ silent meditation" assists in preventing confusion, mind wandering, bringing understanding and wisdom. There are seven basic types of Meditation: Breathing, Visualization, Point [or chakra], Sound [mantra], Movement [mudra], Devotional, and Contemplative. *Wisdom:* enables one to make right decisions based on right thought, and right motivation, so One can take right action in daily living.

As we know "timing" is very important in life. Within the Dharma Wheel of Buddha time there is the Former Day of the Law, some three thousand years ago, the Middle Day of the Law, over two thousand years ago and the present Latter Day of the Law which began approximately 1,100 c.e. The precepts of the Latter Day of the Law are connected to the *Three Great Secret Ways* as defined by the Buddha as: the Object of Practice, the Place where one practices and the Method in which one practices. It is important to *understand that the Precepts and the Practice do not exist apart from each other.*

One who accepts the Buddhist Precepts, taking vows within the *Nichiren* School, may receive a personal mandala called a **Gohonzon.** Has a spiritual space within One's home, recites portions of the Buddha's words called the Liturgy and chants daily for the well being of self and others to help relieve the suffering in ones family, ones community and the world, thereby assisting with peaceful means for Oneself and others. Embracing all three is, in fact, One Unity and not apart from each other. The Chinese scholar *Miao-lo* tells us: *"fusion with the correct object of faith* *will result in great merit. However, if one fuses with an incorrect object, it will never be the seed for attaining enlightenment and Buddhahood even if one believes with utmost sincerity."*

In other words, the precepts teach us that through faith, practice and study we can attain a life condition of merit, but if One chooses wrong thoughts, wrong motivation or takes wrong action there will be no merit. The *Lotus Sutra* teaches us that "everyone" can attain enlightenment in this lifetime as we are and not have to wait for future lifetimes and some other heaven or pure land. In our NOW we practice the Buddhist-way through awareness, breath, visualization, sound and blissfulness. *Nichiren* Buddhists do this primarily through the *Five~In~One~Meditation* the chanting of **Nam~Myoho~Renge~Kyo** which encompasses all of the mentioned ways. Which leads to moments of silent appreciation and Realization and awareness beyond words.

The Precept of Theoretical Teaching

In the *Shakumon* Sutra we find: "this sutra [Lotus Sutra] is difficult to embrace and maintain, but those who uphold it for a prolonged period will find personal joy and will be in the presence of all the Buddhas.... All messengers including *Shakyamuni* and *Nichiren*, clearly state that people can substitute their lack of wisdom by simple faith as a starting point which will lead to actual proof beyond the theory of the doctrine.

The Precept of Essential Teaching

The precept of the *Essential Teaching* in our *Latter Day of the Law* is the fundamental practice of embracing the Law of Cause and Effect and Chanting the sound meditation of *Nam~Myoho~Renge~Kyo* daily. This corresponds to the capacity of persons at the early stages of Buddha practice of "producing even a single moment of faith and understanding" and "rejoicing on first hearing the Lotus Sutra." With six and a half billion people on earth, what are your chances of finding out about the *Lotus Sutra* or of hearing about the Three Time Zones of the Buddha Dharma Wheel? The master Buddhist of Japan *Denygo* [767 - 822] stated: *"If in the Latter Day of the Law there should be persons who keep the precepts, that would be something rare, like a tiger in the marketplace."* ND Here was a Buddhist master talking 500 years into the future.

How fortunate that we live in the times that we do. The average person could not keep the Precepts before the Latter Day of the Law. They involved ten major precepts, forty-eight minor precepts and ten eternal precepts as taught in the *Brahma Net Sutra* and the *Sutra of Jewel-like Acts,* making it unlikely for the average person to accept or practice.

The Diamond Chalice Precept

In the worthy writing or *Gosho* on "Teaching, Practice and Proof" *Nichiren* states: "The five characters of *Myoho-Renge-Kyo,* the heart of the *Honmon* Teachings of the *Lotus Sutra,* contain all the benefits amassed by the beneficial practices and meritorious deeds of all the Buddhas throughout the past, present and future. So, how can this phrase not include the benefits obtained by observing all the Buddha's precepts? Once the practitioner embraces this perfectly-endowed eternal precept, he/she cannot break it, even if he or she should try. It is therefore called the precept of the Diamond Chalice. ND

Through daily practice and following the precepts we can expiate negative karma and produce positive karma leading to wisdom. Each one of us can profoundly assist with peace in our community by practicing the Buddhist philosophy, by practicing the way of caring, compassion, sharing, non-judgement, through right motivation and right action. The Buddhist philosophy starts simply by chanting for self and others each day.

Next, one awakens to the Law of *Cause and Effect* and dedicates a place in the home to practice daily. *Nichiren* taught that the fundamental precept is to chant the all inclusive title of the *Lotus Sutra*, how simple, yet how profound. It is chanted in the ancient sound vibration format in all countries of the world, regardless of country, colour or culture. **Nam-Myoho-Renge-Kyo.** *"Devotion to the infinite, universal Law, of the Buddha's teachings of the Lotus Sutra, thorough the sound of your beautiful voice, originally the voice of the Buddha."*

Through meditation All are enabled easy access to the Universal Law. Through the Precepts, Meditation and Wisdom we make offerings to the Universal Law and receive benefits far beyond what words can express. How wonderful !

Fusion of the Person and the Law

In the Buddhist teachings, the Infinite Eternal Law is perfectly fused with Buddha Wisdom, and Buddha Wisdom is inherent in all things, both sentient and insentient. This is what is called the *Fusion of the Person and the Law,* bringing together objective reality, different people, different personalities with subjective wisdom. We are all human and our connectivity, fusion or conscious contact with the universal Law is "a condition of the highest understanding, vitality and wisdom."

Within the Buddhist philosophy we are taught about many minds-one heart, harmony, and spiritual sustain-ability. In the concept of the Oneness of the Person and the Law, we find acceptance even in life's greatest challenges. *The fusion of our Person and the infinite, eternal, universal Law* can be a difficult concept to master, but going there You will know it! How do we find Oneness in love and hate, in war and peace, in good and evil, causes and conditions, life and death? How do we find Oneness in the diversity of the ten Worlds and the Five lessons: Family, Relationships, Career, Health and Economics. How can we have both Oneness and diversity? The first step is to realize duality as a non factor.

As we now know, the Buddha Dharma has three Treasures, the Buddha, the Law and the Beings. Also, we should understand that the mutual possession of the Three Treasures leads to *Nirvana*, the end of All suffering. Getting this all together is not an easy understanding. However, this is our challenge and a *master key* to our wisdom and personal "enlightenment, just as we are. As a starting place let us consider that all humans exist through dependent origination. Within the human body, there are different organs and energy flows, such as eyes, nose, tongue, ears, hands and feet; blood and nervous energy, all are a part of the Oneness of our body. When we say the people of the country, we mean all the people from every direction, the Oneness of all citizens. We mean in general terms all the people, north, east, south and west. Even though each person has an individual personality and is different in myriad ways, we all share the Oneness of Humanity.

But, how do we live with this Oneness when we see so much history and our present day world acting insanely in so many ways. In society we see the huge gap between the rich and the poor, the powerful and weak, the humble and the arrogant, the greedy and the needy, the wise and the ignorant, the honest and the dishonest. All countries, governments and corporations are made up of people. So, we are forced to admit there are many unenlightened beings that are part of the Oneness. We, for our part, must co-exist through compassion, meditation and prayer. We can then be at peace with ourselves. This will eventually flow to those in our family, community even One's workplace. Compassion means unconditional loving-kindness. We have all seen the bumper stickers that state: "do random acts of kindness." These are Actions of Oneness, kindness renders less stress, a smile, happiness, and forgiveness relieves self and others of suffering.

The Buddha tells us: *"All beings already possess the wisdom to realize their inherent Buddha nature."* This statement shows the Oneness of the Buddha and all other living Beings. The ocean provides the world for fish, the air the world for birds and the earth provides for us all. Our universe has a place for the stars and the planets. Biologically we take care of our living needs by alternately inhaling oxygen and exhaling carbon dioxide. One cannot be without the other, a part of natures Oneness. All things go through the cycle of birth, change and death, a part of the Oneness of the infinite, universal Law, the Buddha and the Beings.

In nature harmony happens according to structure. In humans we have to work at harmony everyday. Dependent origination does not guarantee, harmony and a life filled with only wonderful happenings in our life. Due to our human karma we daily find injustice, social unrest, and continuous wars over people, in the name of religion, land and resources. We find communities, nations and the earth under great stress, and, the earth responds with tsunami's, earthquakes and other natural phenomena complaints against human-kinds faults. *Karma* is universal, not just individual, it applies to All our environment! The buddhist task is to help build spiritual sustain-ability, a positive energy force in the desire for *Kosen Rufu*, peaceful means beyond borders through an active buddhist faith and practice. This action brings greater understanding, social activation, loving kindness and empathy. Take as one small example the women who took the workers of an oil refinery hostage in order to get the corporation to listen to their simple requests for better water, hygiene and electricity. Take for example the millions of people who daily meditate and chant for peace that more people will hear and participate in the Buddha-way of peaceful means.

Oneness Realization ~ *Actuality of the Buddha-way*

As we have shared, Buddha means *awakened*. A Buddha is one who has awakened fully to the true nature of all existence, awakened to the realization that duality blocks harmony, peace and Oneness. This is the *Realization of Non-Duality*. Not good or bad, right or wrong, war or peace. Loving existence within the complexity of all things, through compassion, empathy and grace. One must come to understand the non-duality of all persons, places, objects, and events that take place in life. Each person on their journey through life and death beyond duality, towards the end of all suffering, Nirvana. When we handle the events and challenges that occur daily in life, through wisdom and understanding, with courage, responsibility and faith, peaceful means are ours. All things pass and when one realizes that each event is but a temporary stage in life; there is no duality of good or bad, happiness or sad, just various stages of complexity and change. Coming to realize the profound Oneness of all life, we realize that though we are different in personality, we are all One within humanity. Realizing the deep truth about One's life, seeing the limits of our own perception, we become open to the actuality of the Buddha-way.

On the 28th day of April, 1253 following some twenty years of study at various major centers of learning including: Enryakuji Temple, the seven major temples in Nara, Yakushi-ji Temple, Senyu-ji Temple, To-ji Temple and Tenno-ji Temple, *Nichiren* [13th century, "nichi" sun, "ren" lotus] declared the establishment of the Way for all people to easily attain an understanding of the Oneness of the Person, the Law and the Priesthood. Later in life, reflecting on a method of teaching all the people about the Oneness of the Three Treasures he asked an old priest, "what should I have as an object of worthy respect that all the people will be able to utilize in their seeking nature." The old Priest replied; "Gaze into the 'Pond of the Morning Star.' See yourself as the object of respect." Looking into the pond, it is a wonder to see the reflection became the great mandala *Gohonzon*. I told this to my friend Shunpon-Hoin in Yokawa. Hoin said, "Wonderful, wonderful *Shakyamuni* met with that old priest and directly transferred that. It is respect worthy, respect worthy." *Sacred Writing of Nichiren* Seeking to help people find the actuality of the Buddha-way, he spent his entire life as an envoy of the Lotus Sutra, explaining this profound fundamental practice for all beings. We find in the Worthy Writings [Gosho] "Easy Delivery of a Fortune Child:" *Is there anything brighter than the sun and moon? Is there anything purer than the lotus flower? The Lotus Flower Sutra is the sun and moon and the lotus flower."*

Therefore it is called *Namu~Myoho~Renge~Kyo*, "Sutra of the Lotus Flower Dharma of the Infinite Eternal Law." When we study, meditate, and contemplate, when we seek documentary, theoretical and best yet when we feel and see actual proof in life then the Oneness of all phenomena will be Realized. Realizing this Oneness in name, entity, quality, function and influence, we reach deep comprehension, finding actual proof and a deep understanding of our natural Buddha nature. Congratulations on your seeking spirit!

Summary of Second Sharing Session

We have shared that the universe is subject to a strict Law of *Cause and Effect*. Consequently, the state of one's life is balanced by One's thoughts, motivations and actions which are partners with the Law of Cause and Effect. Buddhists do not believe in some divine God, but rather a natural Law of our universe and the universes beyond. Within the Three Existences of Past, Present and Future, NOW is the most vital element.

We shared the Ten Major tenants or belief system of the Mahayana Buddhist philosophy within the *Mahayana Nichiren* tradition. And, that one of the fundamental methods of practice is through the Five In One, chanting of *Nam~Myoho~Renge~Kyo*. We will share more about this in the next Sharing Session.

We explained that Buddhist practice is made up of Precepts, Meditation and Wisdom. We discovered that practice of the Buddha-way leads to indestructible understanding, realization, peace and happiness.

We had a brief discussion on the Buddhist methods of meditation and prayer and an overview of the two chapters from the Lotus Sutra that is chanted by Nichiren Buddhists in many countries around the world. We will discover more about this later.

We had a discovery of the Fusion of the Person and the infinite universal Law.

We touched on the fact that the *Sutra of the Lotus Flower Dharma of the Infinite Eternal Law* is considered by scholars, academics, and millions of lay believers, to be the Buddha's highest teachings.

The Buddha's teachings have been protected and kept through the Heritage of the Law, by the Priesthood and the Buddhist Sanghas.

Discovering Your Buddha Nature

The Buddha - The Law - The Beings

Sharing Session   THREE OF SEVEN

1] The LOTUS SUTRA ~ The Complete Teaching
2] Nirvana
3] Five In One Meditation ~ Sound Meditation Chanting
4] Introductory Meaning of *NAM* ~ *MYOHO* ~ *RENGE* ~ *KYO*
5] KYO the Merit & Benefit of Sound Meditation ~ Chanting
6] *Juzu* Beads Use & Meaning

The Lotus Sutra ~ *The Whole & Complete Teaching*

It is said that there are 84,000 Buddhist teachings. That is to say there is an answer to all One's quests as well as answers to the **Five Challenges** of life: Family, Relationship, Health, [Physical, Mental & Spiritual,] Career and Economics or Money.

Three Freedoms:

1] Health   2] Happiness   3] Wisdom

Seven Essentials in order to obtain the Three Freedoms*:*

A productive, balanced life on earth, expiating negative karma, producing positive karma with the Realization of the temporary nature of this life. A manifestation of good Health, Physical, Mental & Spiritual. A belief system and understanding how it affects you as well as the people and events in your life. A manifestation of personal power, Right Thought, Right Motivation, and Right Action. A manifestation of empowerment through Chanting, Meditation, Prayer, Contemplation. Devotion to Reflection, Review, Learning, Realization, Wisdom and Enlightenment. Development towards *true-self* for peaceful means, one that enables you to assist others as well as yourself. There is a lot here to meditate on!

Scripture of the Lotus Blossom of the Fine Dharma

"This sutra the Scripture of the Lotus Blossom of the Fine Dharma before which I bow my head, in its single case, with its eight scrolls, twenty-eight chapters, and 69,384 characters, is in each and every one of its characters the true Buddha, who preaches the Law for the benefit of living beings." Tien Tai Chi'I [538 - 597]

Congratulations on being a human who this day is being introduced into the highest of the Buddha's teachings. The *Lotus Sutra* was taught in the last eight years of *Shakyamuni's* earthly existence. Perhaps the most profound statement of the *Lotus Sutra*, is found in the Twenty First Chapter, we find the following statement: *"I have briefly described in this sutra [teaching] all the laws of the Buddha, all the invincible eternal powers of the Buddha, all the secret storehouses of the Buddha and all the profound practices of the Buddha."* Surely, answers to All our Quests. The ancient classic all inclusive title of the *Lotus Sutra* is *Saddharma-pundarika-sutra*, translating into the universal **Myoho~Renge~Kyo**. A first translation is: *"devotion to the eternal infinite universal Law, connecting the Buddha and the Beings, through the teachings of the Buddha Dharma of the Lotus Sutra, through the sound of Your beautiful voice, originally the voice of the Buddha."* The first fourteen chapters are called the *Theoretical* teachings and the latter fourteen the *Essential* teachings. The *Lotus Sutra* integrates all the partial truths revealed in his first forty years of teaching into a perfect whole, and represents the essence and the entirety of the system of Buddhist philosophy that leads to wisdom and enlightenment in here and NOW!

In the first chapter the Buddha's wisdom is instantly recognized as he includes many more entities than human beings. At the assembly of listeners were eighty thousand great bodhisattvas, many gods including *Taishaku* with his entourage of twenty thousand deities, the four heavenly kings, accompanied by ten thousand retainer gods, eight dragon kings, four kings who possessed beautiful voices, four gods of music who subsist on fragrances, four kings of contentious demons, four kings who prey upon dragons, and several local Kings, each with several hundred thousand followers, along with countless other beings, both human and non-human. What an exciting *mythical* gathering when only in today's modern science are we accepting that truly we cannot be alone in the many hundreds of thousands of universes that exist beyond our own. Some 3,000 years ago the Buddha taught a truth which is not limited to human existence alone, rather it encompasses all phenomena in the universe, amongst the billions of galaxies; it is the single great teaching that unites the manifold forms of reality in past, present and future. In the *Second Chapter* we are given the fundamental reason a Buddha appears. "All Buddhas, the World Honoured Ones, make their advent in the world for "one great reason," namely to awaken in all people the Buddha wisdom, to reveal it, to let all Beings know it and enter into it. In other words, a Buddha appears for the sole purpose of enabling all beings to attain the very same enlightenment as a Buddha.

Nirvana

Nirvana like energy and karma has many levels of Being. *Nirvana* translates as *the elimination of All suffering*. With this in mind, we can begin to understand how we can achieve health, happiness and riches in our lives in the here and NOW. In our earlier sessions we shared the major principle of the *"Selection of the Time."* We know from the words of the Lotus Sutra that different times, have different powers of ability. What is important to understand is that all life possesses the same intrinsic Buddha empowerment which simultaneously is permeating the universe itself. Each of our lives is filled with an enormous dynamic energy sufficient to influence even the macrocosm. The living Buddhist philosophy shares the way to tap into this life force and relieve All suffering. It was appearance of *Nichiren* in the 13th century in the present Latter Day of the Law who reawakened the world to the teaching of the *Lotus Sutra* so the predictions of *Shakyamuni* some two thousand two hundred years earlier could be carried out.

In the Second Chapter of the Lotus Sutra, "Expedient Means" we find: *"the wisdom of all Buddhas is infinitely profound and immeasurable. The portal of this wisdom is difficult to understand and difficult to enter. The Buddha has realized the infinite, boundless and unparalleled Law."* This Law refers to the "true aspect of all phenomena." "This reality consists of appearance, nature, entity, power, influence, internal cause, relation, latent effect, manifest effect, and their consistency from beginning to end." These are the Ten Factors. In our time *Nichiren* revealed the distinction between the Buddha Dharma of the Harvest and the Buddha Dharma of Sowing. He re-establishes that *Namu* signifies a simultaneous fusion or two-way interaction: we devote ourselves to, or become One with, the infinite, boundless and unparalleled Law, while at the same time drawing forth infinite energy and wisdom which functions in response to our changing circumstances. Faith and practice constitute the fundamental means by which we become enabled to eliminate our illusions and suffering. We are told that after the Buddha's passing: *"if there is One who hears even a single verse or phrase of the Lotus Sutra and devotes to it even a single moment of rejoicing, on that person too, I confer a prophecy of unexcelled, perfect enlightenment."* We should rejoice on hearing such a prophecy!

In the *Sixteenth Chapter* of the essential teachings we hear: *"listen well and hear the Tathagata's secret and his eternal power."* What we learn is that his "eternal power" is not some supernatural or occult power, but a power latent in all people's lives which each of us can tap into. His secret refers to the three properties of life itself and the eternal power to their functions. The Three properties comprise 1] the property of the Law, 2] the property of Wisdom and 3] the property of Action. A Buddha is not a categorically different being, but a common mortal who manifests Buddhahood from the depths of his or her personal life. A Buddha is simply one who is awakened to his or her own inherent enlightenment, while a common mortal is not. Therefore, there is no essential difference between a common mortal and a Buddha. The pathway to Nirvana is within our Being!

The Four Aspects of Nirvana

The most important aspect of *Nirvana* for us to understand is the word "fusion."

From the early teachings of Nirvana we find pure nirvana or One's pure-nature. Can we see nirvana is part of the fusion of the Person and the Law, that nirvana is in fact already a part of me? Nirvana is that which has cloth, that which takes on matter, we find it in our Seventh Consciousness, still held by earthly desires. Then there is the nirvana of no cloth, free from earthly desires, liberated from matter and materiality. Nirvana that is nowhere and everywhere, no fixed space, spontaneous without intellectual discovery. The nirvana of instant Being, love, compassion, wisdom, floating without floating, free in the infinite, universal Being. Nirvana fused with All that is One, that eternally benefits all sentient or living beings. It is within the realm of Nirvana that we turn our earthly desires into the end of our pain and suffering, into wisdom and enlightenment.

In this sense *Enlightened* does not mean an intellectual understanding, but rather a perception of the ultimate reality of life. Enlightenment occurs when a person actually experiences a sense of Oneness with the Universe and of the eternity of life. Because life does not go beyond the moment, the Buddha expounds the benefit of even a single moment's pure joy. Much of this will become clearer as we study the principle of *Ichinen Sanzen*, and the mutual possession of the *Ten Worlds* through the *Ten Factors*.

The Buddha Wisdom in our *Latter Day of the Law* aims at being practical, useful and applicable. In short this living philosophy is the *Buddha Dharma of Actuality and Sowing*. The promise is that All can reach Nirvana.

The Five In One Meditation

> ***Though a cave may be dark for a thousand years, bring a lamp into it and lo and behold the cave is no longer dark." Ancient Saying***

The lamp of Buddhist philosophy is the concept of Oneness. The fusion of the Person and the Law, the oneness of life and it's environment, the oneness of body and mind, the oneness of birth and death. We cannot separate the individual from the community, the community from the country, we cannot separate the self from the environment.

Seven Classic Types of Meditation

1] breath 2] visualization 3] point [chakra] awakening 4] sound [getha] chanting 5] movement [mudra] yoga, Tai Chi 6] awareness and 7] direct essence of contemplation

Ten Qualities of Meditation

1] daily practice 2] sincerity 3] self-respect 4] simplicity 5] discipline 6] correct place 7] non attachment [no doubt] 8] contentment 9] faith 10] patience

Three Stages of Meditation

First Stage:
A feeling of calmness, comfort, thoughts passing through, somewhat aware, peaceful

Second Stage:

Non attachment, no specific thinking, acceptance, inner joy, bliss, peaceful Being, Awareness.

Third Stage:
Oneness beyond the senses of touch, smell, hearing, seeing, feeling, Seventh Consciousness and higher

Five In One ~ *Sound Meditation* ~ *Chanting*

With the use of *Sound Meditation*, we bring Five main steps of Meditation into One. Chanting forces breathing, straightens the chakras, uses sound and visualization, is done becoming aware, leading to blissful contemplation. Meditation works to establish One's *true self* with an indestructible strength of character enabling one to understand that life is change and temporary. One must be strong to survive all challenges and lessons from the worlds of *Learning* and *Realization*. When we attain this level of knowing and attain the state of *non back sliding* then we come to understand that happiness and suffering are One and the same, that good and bad are not different, that life and death are one circle of Dharma. That there is no life of duality. At one moment we are happy, at another we are sad, at another we are filled with joy, then suddenly with pain. Such are the human characteristics of life on our planet. The *Ten Worlds* as expressed in the Middle Day of the Law, by *Tien Tai Chi'I* are in constant motion on the Dharma Wheel of Life. We call our world the *saha* or world of endurance. So, gathering the *awareness* is very difficult. Attaining the silence not easy. Yet the ancient Zen poet tells us: "The perfect Way [Tao] is without difficulty. It is also said that "one glorious day on earth, is worth a thousand days in the other worlds." In other words it is up to each of us to practice towards perfection.

Meditation of the Thousand Ways

Meditation then is a balance of awareness, concentration and energy. When we start meditating, it becomes clear that everything is changing moment to moment, as the mind races from place to place like a ping pong ball in action. Our thought patterns change and challenge, the body shifts and demands attention, we find it hard to be still, calm yet energized with the ability to concentrate with mindfulness. Naturally, our meditations will be appropriate to the mood or condition we are in at the moment of practice. Our disposition will be determined by our posture, our approach, our attitude, our view, and by desire. The main point is that one must practice every day regardless of the kind of day we have had. Chanting through frustration or anger, chanting through sadness or sorrow, chanting with joy and happiness, chanting for health or wealth but chanting everyday communicating with the universal Law. This is the *Meditation of a Thousand Ways* bringing the *Five Desired Powers* of compassion, empathy, understanding, mindfulness [beyond intellect] and vanishing doubt, eternal answers to life's quest.

The important thing in practising meditation is not to worry about the mental state you are in, or whether you are doing it correctly or not; just do it sincerely. You will achieve personal empowerment with practice. All our meditative life force vibrations go out into the universe, are heard and are responded to. This is why we chant to the *Shoten Zenjin* or universal energy guardians, protectors of those who practice the Buddha-way, that they may be nourished by Our energy force and meditations. Treating One's meditation with the same attitude as if our most cherished, loved family member or friend were coming for a visit, then even if we are in a bad state of mind, our energy flow will alter.

Sound Meditation ~
Chanting of Nam ~ Myoho ~ Renge ~ Kyo

On April 28, 1253 a new messenger, the Buddha of the Latter Day of the Law, a manifestation of the eternal Buddha, *Nichiren Daishonin** chanted Nam~Myoho~ Renge~Kyo and pronounced this sound meditation as the primary practice for the times. In his writing "The One Essential Phrase" the Buddha explains: *Nam-Myoho-Renge-Kyo is only one phrase, but it contains the essence of the entire sutra." "Everything has its essential point, and the heart of the Lotus Sutra is its title, Nam~Myoho~Renge~Kyo. Truly, if you chant this in the morning and evening, you are correctly reading the entire Lotus Sutra..... Thus if you ceaselessly chant Daimoku, you will be continually reading the Lotus Sutra."* Nichiren Daishonin

Meaning of NAM~MYOHO~RENGE~KYO

It means *relationship,* the essence of communication with One's inner self and the cosmos. It is an all inclusive title that cannot be understood by verbal or emotional definition alone. To do so would be like trying to pick up all the single grains of sand along the shores of the Pacific Ocean. It is our human connection with the infinite universal Law the true entity of life permeating all phenomena. The chanting of *Nam~Myoho~Renge~Kyo* connects One's present life to all past and future existence. If one does not believe that life is eternal then it makes no sense at all.

NAM or NAMU: means "devotion or I take refuge in the Buddha." *Namu* signifies a simultaneous fusion of the Person and the Eternal Law. The entity of eternal life essence, it is the Law enabling all humans to draw forth wisdom, energy and life-force. The inclusion of this "getha" or sound meditation provides personal empowerment through a meditation of universal value, *conscious communication* with all phenomena.

MYOHO: *Myo* = eternal and wonderful *Ho* = law, literally wonderful, eternal Law. Eternal Law indicates beyond common intellect, unfathomable. The entity our eternal life essence. The law of *Cause* and *Effect* eternal change, existence in constant flux, emptiness, the void and complete wholeness.

RENGE, *Lotus* Blossom or flower. The lotus blooms and seeds at the same time. This is a mystery and a miracle of life. This is a Buddhist way of showing the simultaneity of cause and effect. We learn in the *Totai Renge,* "From the muddy water comes the beautiful flower, no matter how dirty one's life there is beauty there." The Master Teacher, *Tien Tai Chi'I* **** in his *Hokke Gengi* states: "Now the name *renge* is not intended as a symbol for anything..... the teaching expounded in the Lotus Sutra is pure and undefiled and explains the subtleties of Cause and Effect. The name *renge* or lotus flower has been given to this teaching. This name designates the true entity of the Lotus Sutra, and is not a simile or figurative term."

Kyo, sound of your beautiful voice, originally the sound of the Buddha's voice. Kyo is sound meditation, chanting, *"conscious communication"* so that we may transform past negative karma into a bright NOW and a future of freedom and happiness. In a broad sense it encompasses the activities of all living beings and all phenomena in our universe. The Chinese character for *kyo* meant a warp of cloth, symbolizing the connection of life, past, present and future. *Kyo* also symbolizes the *pathway to enlightenment*.

Through "sound meditation ~ chanting" of *Nam~Myoho~Renge~Kyo* every individual can manifest their Buddha nature and experience universal harmony in his or her daily life. Just as complicated mathematical formulas are unreadable to the untrained mind, so are the secrets revealed in the spiritual aspect of sound meditation. Chanting or sound meditation in accord with our momentary life force has an effect on the human body, mind and spirit.

Chanting NAM~MYOHO~ RENGE~KYO is *"conscious communication"* with the Oneness of the infinite eternal Law so that we may find intimate growth, peaceful means for ourselves and assist in helping others. It is far beyond egos, intellect and personalities.

---

*   Nichiren [Sun-Lotus] Daishonin [Great Sage] Buddha of the Latter Day of the Law, 1222-1282
**   Lotus Sutra, Kumarajiva 406 Translation of the Buddha's highest teachings
***   Daimoku, sound meditation, getha chanting, title of writing
****   Tien Tai Chi'I, 538 - 597 Master Scholar, Great Teacher, Priest in Middle Day of the Law

Merit & Benefit of Five In One, "getha" Chanting

As we have seen, Buddhists know that there are three pathways of Faith, Practice and Study. And that the primary *Mahayana* practice is *conscious communication* with the infinite, universal Law. This is done through One's chanting and voice repetition, setting up powerful energy vibrations. This sound meditation is chanted each day by millions of people throughout many countries, it is the primary practice that leads us to silent wonder. But you ask, how can the repetition of a single phrase answer prayers and questions, cause expiation of negative karma, and produce personal miracles. What happens when we chant?

What Happens When We Chant ?

Several years ago a research study at the University of Boston proved scientifically what the Buddha taught some 3,000 years ago. Sound meditation and chanting sets up wonderful brain waves that can produce balance, bliss, calmness and peaceful reality. Through chanting the all inclusive title of the *Lotus Sutra*, we invite all kinds of good fortune into our life. When it comes to the benefit to be gained from chanting *Nichiren* tells us: "If only you chant *Nam-Myoho-Renge-Kyo*, then what offense could fail to be eradicated? What blessing could fail to come?" ND

Chanting is made up of three phases: 1] the sound, word or words 2] the motivation or sense   3] the manifestation. Chanting is therefore, not just about the words; the force is in their audible pronunciation which produces vibration. We must take care never to allow our thoughts, motivations and actions deteriorate into disrespect. Our words, voice, speech and emotions work together. *Our universe is made up of pure energy.* Tapping into this energy is why sound meditation is an important personal empowerment.

Where Do Our Thoughts Come From

Getha, mantra, words and symbol formulas consisting of a short group of select words sounds or syllables which affect the mind, body and spirit through energy. *Manipura*: power of the spoken word, language thought. *Pingala*: energy channel on the right side of the body, *Ida*: Energy channel on the left side of the body, *Susumna*: Central channel of the spine. This is the nervous and life force flow of One's potential meditations. A person speaks at about four hundred and fifty words a minute, the other person thinks at about sixteen hundred words a minute, time to seemingly be doing several other things besides listening. But even more amazing is the fact that at any one millisecond there are literally millions of activating nerve impulses going on in the cortex of the brain. Through our will power we select that which we choose as thought or let it pass simply as energy and potential messengers of anger, sight, hearing, stress, sleep, love, joy, bliss.

The Body's Nervous System

Our body's nervous system is divided into three main parts: the central nervous system [brain and spinal cord] the peripheral nervous system, including the *receptor* and the *afferent* impulses, and the third aspect of the hidden spiritual energy force *within*. Herein lies our secret power. With practice the powers of chanting will energize, protect, and respond to our body's needs and our earthly desires for physical, mental and spiritual Health. At the higher levels of consciousness we achieve *a feeling beyond words*. With practice One achieves *"mantra consciousness,"* a peaceful, blissful harmony coming from our meditations.

When we chant, we set in motion electromagnetic vibrations that go out into our universe. These vibrations are felt and responded too as Guide Teachers have known for thousands of years and as our scientists have proven in more recent years. Perhaps, we can appreciate that just as complex mathematical formulas are not understood by the untrained mind, so too the higher and eternal reality of our Five In One *Sound Meditation*. *Einstein* and other scientists have discovered our universe is governed by this electromagnetic impulse system. As humans we are a part of this vital universal process. When we sincerely chant repetitious sounds, we set off energy vibrations, positive wave impulses. Chanting sends out vibrations to the Infinite Consciousness which has no beginning and no ending, yet catches every vibration in the same manner that a ray of sunshine falls equally on everything under its power and reach.

One's Meditation, prayer and chanting are a direct bridge between self, and the life energy in harmony with the universal Oneness, call it your Higher Power, God, or whatever you choose, it is the bridge that crosses over from our world of endurance to the world of peaceful means. *This is the secret power that dwells within us.* It is not so important how fast or how slow you chant, or even how correctly you chant but rather the *sincere* manner in which you approach your spiritual Health. As you chant simply let go! This is not an intellectual exercise, it is the Way of *conscious communication* with the eternal, universal Law.

Finally understand that the chanting manifests itself in three ways, through sound, senses and manifestation within the Law of Cause and Effect. How wonderful!

"This Meditation is a Personal Gift to One's Self" HL

Vow of the Guardians of Energy and Light

In the *Lotus Sutra*, the *Shoten Zenjin* or Guardians of the universe have sworn to protect those who chant, follow the Buddha's teachings and seek enlightenment. Therefore, we can believe chanting has truly profound meaning and function.

Spiritual leaders tell us the seven syllables of 1] Nam   2] Mu   3] Myo   4] Ho   5] Reng   6] Ge 7] Kyo; signify the five major principles of designation, entity, quality, function and teaching.

The use of sound exists throughout every belief system in the universe since the beginning of time. The magic of sound is a miracle in itself. The fact that we have been given a Way to correspond with creation itself is most wonderful and life empowering!

We are reminded that this chanting of *Nam~MyoHo~Renge~Kyo*, will transform the three paths of earthly desires, karma and suffering, into the three virtues of the spiritual body, wisdom and freedom. Through chanting, we are connecting life and environment, body and mind, entity and function. Thus, through the magic, glory and wonder of sound **KYO** , we can manifest actual proof of universal wonder.

We can raise our human consciousness to the higher worlds and be assured that we can attain enlightenment in our present form, on this *earthly world of endurance.* Chanting brings together, person and universe, person and earth, person and environment, energy and light. This is *the invincible eternal power of the Buddha, the secret storehouse of the Buddha and the profound practice of the Buddha.*

Know that it is good, worthy and respectful, repaying our debt of gratitude through our daily offerings to the Buddha's and Shoten Zenjin of the Ten Directions who are nourished by our offerings.

The Significance of Buddha *JUZU** Beads

To understand the meaning of the beads is to begin to understand the depth of Buddha wisdom and our reason for expressing gratitude to the Three Great Secret Laws and the Three Treasures.

Beads have been used for thousands of years by all faiths as an aid to worshiping. They act as an agent to bring comfort, take away tension and help with concentration. As an object of interest they say to others; tell me what is the purpose of your beads ? *Juzu* beads have been used by Buddhists for thousands of years. They are used whenever we approach meditation and prayer. For many, they are a part of our clothing used whenever and wherever we meditate and pray. The number of the beads is set at 108 regular beads. The number 108 stands as a symbol for the number of earthly desires. It is through our desires that we humans are given the ability to turn earthly desires into enlightenment.

The origins of the *Juzu* beads is explained in a sutra called the *Mokugenji Sutra*. Once there was a king called King Virudhaka. He approached the Buddha saying: "My country is small and my people have been plagued by frequent epidemics and inflation of grain prices for many years. Because of this, I never have a moment of peace. And the trove of Laws that the Buddha teaches is indeed vast, it would be impossible for me to practice all of his teachings. My wish is that you would reveal the essence of what I need do to practice the universal Law."

To this the Buddha replied, "Dear King, if you wish to transform your earthly desires, then you should string together one-hundred and eight nuts of the mokugenshi tree and carry them with you at all times as you go about your daily affairs. Concentrate your mind as you chant "I submit myself to the Buddha, I submit myself to the Law, I submit myself to the Sangha" moving one nut each time you finish chanting this phrase. When you have finished this austerity 200,000 times, your body and mind will find ease, and if you have been unselfish and without deceit, upon your death you will be reborn in a heavenly realm where you will be happy and be always at peace." This story reminds us that beads assist with awareness, concentration and practice we should treat them with obvious respect.

Thus we learn to find comfort in our beads. The Buddha of the Latter Day of the Law, *Nichiren Daishonin*, is shown in many portraits holding his beads. So you might ask, what does he have to say about beads. Actually, since Buddhists have carried beads as a matter of course for many thousands of years, there is little reference to them by Nichiren. In the "Teachings on the Precepts" he says, "Always treat the *Juzu* with the same respect as you would a Buddha." This is a pretty direct manner of saying show respect.

Significance of the Shape of Our Beads

1] The form of the Beads signifies the five characters of *Myo*, the wonder of life

2] The roundness of the beads represents the eternal principle of the laws of nature.

3] The circle and space inside the beads represents eternal *enlightenment*

4] The two large beads at each end represent the stability of the Middle Pathway

5] The two tassels represent duality, *male and female, reality and wisdom*

6] The three tassels represent past, present and future, and the Three Treasures

7] The four small oblong beads signify the four leaders of the Bodhisattvas of the Earth Jogyo, Element of Fire, True Self;

Muhengo, Element of Air, Eternity of Life. Anryugyo, Element of Earth, Happiness and Jyogo, Element of Water, Purity of Life

8] The 30 beads on the five tassels represents the 3,000 realms of a single life-moment, the instant of NOW, Ichinen Sanzen

9] The end *Vases* hold blessings and benefits of our life, whether we see them or not

10] The five white tassels symbolize the desire for *Kosen Rufu*, peaceful means that all suffering may be alleviated through faith, practice and study of the Buddha-way

Buddhist Purpose and Function

Through faith, practice and study Buddhists make *Four Universal Vows*. They are to share our practice to help eliminate all suffering, to eradicate negative karma and produce positive karma, beyond the duality of negative and positive, to master the teachings, and to seek enlightenment in this lifetime. The beads are a tool of comfort and inquiry to assist us in our goals.

Nam~Myoho~Renge~Kyo..........
Nam~Myoho~Renge~Kyo..........

*	Juzu, small round nuts of the Mokugenshi tree.
**	Three Great Secret Laws = the object of worship, the method, and the high sanctuary or place One practices
***	Three Treasures = the Buddha, the Law, the Beings, the Buddha the Law, the Sangha, The Buddha, the Law, the Priesthood

Summary of Third Sharing Session

We shared that of all the Buddhas teachings the scripture of the Lotus Sutra was developed after Shakamuni's passing. It became respected as his highest teachings due to the predictions, clarity, and Oneness doctrine.

We shared that there are 84,000 Buddhist teachings, Five major life Challenges, Three Freedoms and Seven Essentials for attaining wisdom and enlightenment just as we are. We found some interesting ideas on Oneness and the fusion of our Person with the infinite eternal universal Law.

We learned that Meditation is a balance between awareness and energy. We learned that there are seven basic types of Meditation. We shared that the practical application of *Sound Meditation* is inclusive with other meditations of breathing, visualization, awareness, and contemplative silence.

We acknowledged the vital life force of energy and light, the *Shotzen Zenjin* and how they give us contact with life's Five Major Principles of designation, entity, quality, function and teaching

In Realizing that within the Meditation of a Thousand Ways, One may attain the Five Desired Powers of understanding, non judgement, compassion, non doubt and mindfulness or awareness we found the heart of wisdom!

We had an opportunity to see the significance of the Buddha *Juzu* Beads. Beads have been used for thousands of years by all faiths as an aid to concentration.

We shared that in the Twenty First Chapter of the *Lotus Sutra*, is the following profound statement: *"I have briefly described in this sutra [teaching] all the laws of the Buddha, all the invincible eternal powers of the Buddha, all the secret storehouses of the Buddha and all the profound practices of the Buddha."* There is much here to reflect and contemplate on as you grow in your knowledge and Discovery of Your Buddha Nature. Congratulations on your seeking spirit!

Discovering Your Buddha Nature

YOUR NOTES

The Buddha - The Law - The Beings

Sharing Session   FOUR OF SEVEN

1] Ten Factors – How the Universe Works
2] Ten Worlds – How the Dharma Wheel of Life Works
3] Twelve Links of Causation - Suffering or Happiness
4] NOW, *Momentary Life Force* ICHINEN SANZEN

Ten Factors That Govern Our Universe

In this sharing session One may find a life changing moment! One of the reasons that the Buddha's teachings have finally reached our shores is that it is based on a "living philosophy of life" with explanations of how life works in One's daily struggle. In this Session we bring together the way in which the Four Noble Truths and the Eightfold Path of *Theravada* Buddhist thought can be brought together with the complete teachings of the Enlightenment doctrine.

As we have seen earlier, there are two major schools of Buddhist thought, *Theravada* and *Mahayana*. Theravada is the Buddha's early teachings. He taught people to think for themselves, remembering that until fairly recently [two three hundred years] the average person was not schooled in the same way we are Now. *Theravada* Sutra's are not untrue, but as the Buddha explained were preparatory doctrine. *Mahayana*, the Buddha's final teachings taught in the last eight to ten years of his life, more difficult to understand, more complete and the Buddha says so.

The Chinese scholar *Tien-Tai Chih'I* 538-597 c.e. spent his life devoted to the comparative classification of all of the Buddha's teachings. Organizing the Buddhist sutras into five periods and eight teachings to clarify their relative timing and position. After thirty years of scholarly work on all the various Sutra's and Buddhist teachings Tien- Tai devoted the last twenty years of his life defining Shakyamuni's highest teachings found in the doctrine of the *Lotus Sutra,* this is the *Scripture of the Lotus Blossom of the Fine Dharma.* **Tien-Tai Ch'I's** major life works are contained in the "*Words and Phrases of the Lotus, Profound Meaning of the Lotus* and *Great Concentration and Insight,*" refuting earlier doctrinal classifications. More about this in the Part Two of our sharing.

Ten Factors ~ *How the Universe Works*

The *Ten Factors* relate to one of three principles of Buddhist understanding, principles clarifying life's entity and functions. The Ten Factors are common to all life in any of the *Ten Worlds*. The first three factors are the *appearance, nature,* and *entity* of life. These three correspond, respectively, to life's physical aspects, spiritual aspects, and the entity which gives rise to and sustains both. The next six are *power, influence, internal cause, relation, latent effect*, and *manifest effect* all functions of life. Lastly the principle which maintains them all in harmony is called *consistency from beginning to end*.

The Ten Factors of life are an analysis of the unchanging aspects of life common to all earthly changing phenomena. The Ten Factors are found in the *Expedient Means,* Second Chapter of the *Lotus Sutra. The wonder, magic and hope that is given in the Ten Factors is the explanation for the first time that since the Ten Factors are common to ALL phenomena or existence, there can be no fundamental distinction between a Buddha and a common mortal.* The Ten Worlds express the differences among phenomena, while the *Ten Factors* describe the pattern of existence common to all phenomena. For example, both the world of Hell and Buddhahood, different as they are, have the Ten Factors in common.

NOW, let's discuss these **TEN FACTORS** through everyday examples in our life.

1] *Nyo ze so* = **Appearance**, the material aspects of our life ie; the car we drive, the home we live in, the clothing we choose to wear. The outside appearance of our life.

2] *Nyo ze sho* = **Nature**, our personality, the wisdom we have gained in living, our self-esteem or lack of it, the full nature of our Being

3] *Nyo ze tai* = **Entity**, Body and Mind combined, the essence of Health, who we are, the manifestation of life as we are today, our present *life force* through body and mind.

4] *Nyo ze riki* = **Power**, interesting that the Buddha would name "power" as a factor and here the meaning of power has to do with our vital energy, our *life force* in relation to our positive or negative energy that gives us the power to live within the life-force we give it.

5] *Nyo ze sa* = **Influence,** in this Factor we now add our spiritual nature to that of the mind and body. Now we have both the physical and the spiritual nature of Being made manifest. Now our creation is whole. Now we can be born!

6] *Nyo ze in* = **Inherent Cause**, our *Karma.* A simple translation of Karma means Action. It is a subject for much study, within the Ten Factors, we realize our *karma* as a work in progress. Later through the *Ten Worlds* we come to know through our suffering or happiness how much karma we have *expiated*. How much slander and incorrect life practice we have dealt with correctly. The process is to give thanks for our suffering and see it as an opportunity to grow, and realize we can improve in our way of thinking, decision making and actions. Understanding that we are responsible for ALL our thoughts, motivations and actions. The joy is in knowing we can turn our *negative karma, into positive karma.* We do this through *faith, practice and study.*

7] *Nyo ze en* = **External Cause**, here is the effect of how we re-act to the *Ten Worlds*. This is where we see the proof of our practice. Are we making right choices? Is our motivation correct in the actions we take, the decisions we make? Of the three kinds of proofs in Buddhist practice [documentary, theoretical, and actual] It is through Actual proof that we are enabled to know two things. First is our practice correct? Second, are we willing to expiate all our negative karma, here and now in this lifetime so we can attain more time in the higher worlds of Rapture [Heaven], Learning, Realization, Bodhisattva and Buddhahood, rather

than in the lower worlds of Hell, Animality, Anger, Hunger and Humanity?

8] *Nyo ze ka* = **Latent Effect**, where we awaken a cause. In living and through our suffering and illnesses we know, through our pain, that all is not right. *Latent effect* allows us to awaken or look within to see the cause of our pain. We do this through the *Worlds of Learning* and *Realization*. Again, it is through *Right Thought, Right Motivation* and *Right Action*, that we can expiate our negative karma, ie: lack of money, lack of a healthy relationship, lack of a good career, loss of a loved one, physical or mental illness, etc. Through the factor of *latent effect*, we can challenge ourselves, awaken to our needs and earthly desires, make positive changes in our life, seek wisdom and enlightenment.

9] *Nyo ze ho* = **Manifest Effect**, is the perceivable, or seen result of our actions. Someone is unhealthy and overweight, decides to do something about it and loses a large amount of weight and everyone says wow, what a difference, and you say, yes and I feel so much better. Or our self - esteem is very low and we think others are judging us or talking about us all the time. So we decide to get professional help and do a major *daimoku** campaign. In time others notice that you smile a lot more, you are not so shy, you compliment others on their health because you are now well enough to love your-self and you can more easily love others. These are simple examples of *manifest effect*. The results are perceivable to you and possibly others, as you live in your changed circumstances, once again practical proof of your faith, practice and study.

10] *Nyo ze honmak kukyo to* = **Consistency from beginning to end**. Here is the inscrutable essence of the universe, the perfect fusion of objective reality *kyo* and subjective reality *chi* the mutual possession of the Buddha of absolute freedom, the eternal manifestation of the Ten Worlds, the embodiment of *Ichinen Sanzen*, and the Oneness of the Person and the Law.

As we work through the various aspects of how our Universe works we are able to *Realize* strong faith. For some this is one of the difficult areas of acceptance, particularly if One has had previous bad life experiences around religion and faith. The good news is we will see results in our life. Acceptance with knowledge and research brings wisdom.

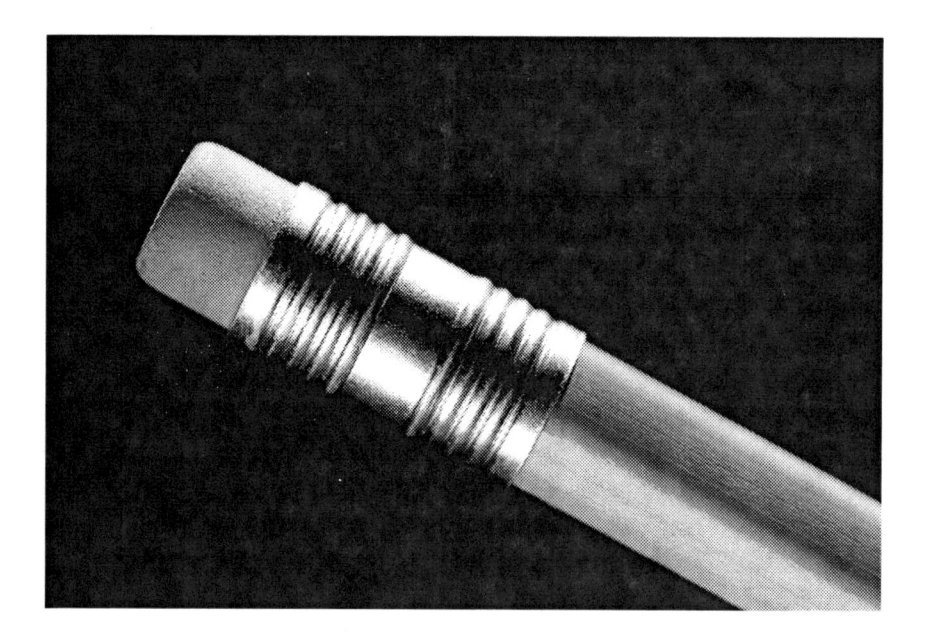

Ten Worlds ~ *How the Dharma Wheel of Life Works*

When something happens to please us we are happy. When we are embarrassed by someone we may first feel humbled and then angry. When someone close dies, we may suffer the loss for a long time. When a child is born, most show love, compassion and gratitude. When we intuitively "know" a truth we realize and grow. Within the living philosophy of Buddha Dharma [wisdom teachings] the Great Teacher, Scholar, Priest *Tien Tai Chi'I* [538-597] explained this as ten life conditions which we as humans manifest from moment to moment.

The Ten Worlds work within the structure of the Ten Factors of all phenomena within our universe. The Ten Factors and Ten Worlds work within the mutual possession of three thousand realms in a single moment of life; *Ichinen Sanzen* each and all a particle of the Oneness of our universe, the Moment of NOW.

Four Lowest Life Conditions

Hell A life condition of no freedom, a state of extreme suffering, the pain of one's negative karma, one of destructive tendencies. Symbolically the documentary texts [Sutras] say that the variety of Hells include eight major [hot] hells, eight cold hells and sixteen minor hells.

Hunger A life state in which one is controlled by greed, desire for power, control, money, fame, always searching never satisfied or at peace. One in this state may suffer from physical and mental disease. Hungry souls are always craving, miserable and use the Law for evil purposes.

Animality A life condition governed by instinct, a general term for animals. A life factor of survival, ego superiority, foolishness and no sense of reason or morality, the struggle for existence. One in this state looks to take advantage of others. It manifests in those not yet awakened to their Buddha nature.

Anger A life condition of selfish ego. In the first volume of T'ien Tai's *Maka Shikan* one reads, "He who is in the world of Anger, motivated by the warped desire to be better than everyone, is forever belittling others and exalting himself. He is like a hawk sweeping the sky in search of prey. He may outwardly display benevolence, righteousness, propriety, wisdom and good faith, and even possess a rudimentary moral sense, but his or her heart remains in *shura*." [anger] When we get angry we are hardly in control of our being, we are in a low world of life condition. We may be angry for seconds, minutes, hours or years living in a negative karmic way.

Middle Pathway

Humanity The World of Tranquility. Buddha Dharma defines a human being as a creature in the world of Humanity. *Manushya* is from the ancient Sanskrit "a creature who thinks." As a human we have the ability of being in any of the Ten Worlds by our mutual possession of the Ten Factors and the Three Realms of the Five Components of Life: form, perception, conception, volition and consciousness. The realm of living beings and the realm of the environment are connected. As suggested by the world of tranquility this should be a life condition of reason, hope, passion, right thinking, right motivation and right action.

Heaven A life condition of joy or rapture. It is said that there are 28 heavens in the World of Heaven, six in the world of desire, 28 heavens in the world of form and four in the world of formlessness. In our humanly higher heavens we experience the light of love, in the mid heavens the world of well being, health and general happiness. In the lower heavens we experience a gratefulness for food, friends, nature and pleasure experienced. When we are caught up in the lower worlds, too often the World of Heaven is fleeting or too brief; we should recognize it when we hold it and realize we have the ability to change our negative karma to a positive One, giving us more earth time in the higher worlds.

The Six Worlds from Hell through Heaven are called the Six Lower Pathways and being in them is governed by our external events and karma. Each pathway is summoned by our life condition at the moment. Our habits formed over time. We are born into this world with one of the Worlds as our major factors, contained within our karma from past lifetimes.

Then through the higher worlds of *Learning* and *Realization* we come to understand that if we do not have the good fortune to be in the higher worlds we can change that through personal growth study and practice expiating negative karma, creating positive karma.

Four Noble Worlds

Learning In our educated times the World of Learning makes immediate sense, but for thousands of years the average person was not allowed schooling or knowledge. Only a very few were taught the "secrets" of knowledge, research, and what we have come to call in our times "science." The World of Learning is where one seeks knowledge based on the ideas, concepts, teachings of others through self development.

Realization Knowing, intuition without doubt, truth as it is for Oneself. Sometimes, it may be recognition of something brought forward from our past, in search of lasting truth along the Buddha Middle pathway within. Sometimes, it is a moment of truth, NOW. We all have these moments, but do we stop to Meditate, Contemplate and blissfully give thanks for this knowing, this Realization?

Bodhisattva *Bodhi* means = buddha wisdom, *sattva* means= sentient beings. Bodhisattvas practice courage, compassion, empathy, respectfulness and helpfulness toward self and others. It is said the eternal Bodhisattvas take four great vows: 1] to carry all people over their suffering enabling them to realize their Buddha nature 2] to banish all unbalanced earthly desires, 3] to master the Worlds of Learning and Realization and 4] to attain Enlightenment thereby being further able to help others.

Buddhahood   The life condition of absolute happiness and freedom, truthfulness, right and universal knowledge, clarity and excellent conduct; without illusion, with boundless wisdom, great power, virtue and competence; an awakened one, with wisdom and virtue, One who wins the respect and approval of others due though their beneficial behavior achieved in our *saha* world of endurance; an *Enlightened Being* or other universal creature.

"Mutual Possession" ~ Inter-dependent Life Condition

The Buddha *Shakyamuni* in his final teachings taught that the Ten Worlds are not actual places but rather potential life conditions inherent in each sentient being. The concept clearly helps us to understand why one moment we may be in the world of Anger and very soon after in the World of Happiness. At any moment, one of them will be manifest and the other nine sleeping. Through *karmic* action, change is constant, reflecting the temporary nature of all life moment by moment.

The concept of **Mutual Possession** teaches that each of the Ten Worlds is a particle of all ten worlds within it. This principle means that the *reality of life is not fixed, only temporary.* The *Maka Shikan* states, "*Each of the Ten Worlds is endowed with all the others.*" The mutual possession explains the interrelationship of the Ten Worlds in connection with the Ten Factors and the principle of *Ichinen Sanzen*.

Each life condition resides in a latent or dormant state. The human condition is different when we are awake than when we are asleep, but the conditions are not separated. Our life condition changes from moment to moment. We are born and take on certain tendencies, personalities, traits; this is known as the "*core life person.*" Some are born mainly in the World of *Anger*, others the World of *Heaven*, others the World of

Hunger, etc. Being born a human delivers us onto one of the main World conditions, then from day one our destiny is our determination.

How wonderful to realize that we can become more, be more compassionate, learn to give, meditate and study to become wise and awaken our Buddha nature to an *enlightened* state of being, assisting our-self and others.

It is important to remember in the living philosophy of Buddha Wisdom that *"enlightenment is not an eternal or transcendental state, as many might assume. Rather it is a condition of the highest wisdom, vitality and good fortune wherein the individual can shape his or her destiny, find fulfillment in daily activities, and come to understand his or her purpose in being alive."* ND

The Twelve-linked Chain of Causation ~
Harmony or Suffering

From the historical Buddha's early teachings we find The *Twelve-Linked Chain of Causation* a central theme of spiritual sustain-ability or inter-dependent manifestation. Modern day scientists are once again discovering how time and space work inter-dependently, how all things in the universe are actually particles of a whole picture and not just separate entities. We as individuals must realize we are not whole without family, friends, lovers, without challenges in our health, on career and economics or money.

Over twenty six hundred years ago the Buddha explained how the universe within our body and mind are inter-dependent. We may ask from time to time, where do my thoughts come from? What is the source of my "inner being?" How do the stars live and die? Why do the tides ebb and flow so consistently? What is the "origin" of life and death?

In fact, this is a central theme of Buddhist Dharma in both the *Theravada* and *Mahayana* Buddhist doctrine. This doctrine shares the principle of *the way in which occurring phenomena comes into being through various circumstances*. It teaches that all phenomena are temporary, constantly living or dying, through the Law of Sowing, Maturing and Harvest, being born, changing and becoming extinct. It teaches us that this is not an accident, it is the Law whereby all things change in a fixed manner due to a fixed set of circumstances. It teaches us that all is mutually inter-dependent eternally.

Inter-Dependent Relationship

This early Buddhist doctrine shows the causal relationship between ignorance and suffering. *Shakyamuni* Buddha is said to have taught this principle to teach people how to avoid suffering in old age as they neared the portal of what we call death. The first link is 1] ignorance which 2] causes action [including karmic influence] 3] action causes consciousness 4] consciousness causes name and form; 5] name and form cause the six sense organs 6] the six sense organs and energy forces cause contact 7] contact causes sensation 8] sensation causes desire 9] desire causes attachment 10] attachment causes existence 11] existence causes birth 12] birth leads to old age and death.

NOTHING exists independently. As we have seen in the study of the *Ten Worlds* and the *Ten Factors,* everything has a mutual inter-relationship. The teaching is one to help us to eliminate all our suffering. In the *Daibisasha Ron* sutra, the Twelve Linked Chain of Causation is viewed as particles of all three existences, past, present and future.

Ignorance and action are together interpreted as the cause one has made in a past lifetime; consciousness through sensation is the effect of our present lifetime, desire, attachment and existence as the cause in our present life; and birth, old age and what we call death, as the effect in the next life.

If we can understand this then we get the whole Buddhist concept of "emptiness", the "void" or "Ku." The principle is really not that difficult, nothing exists alone, by itself or for itself independently, Eternity is inter-connected and mutually possessed.

Buddhists understand the *Four Noble Truths,* which clarifies the cause of suffering and how to eliminate pain and unhealthiness. 1] existence will have suffering 2] suffering is caused by selfishness 3] the elimination of selfish craving brings about the cessation of suffering 4] there is a pathway which one can achieve, to end personal suffering

The *Eight-Fold Pathway* the practice to eliminate suffering: 1] right views 2] right thinking 3] right speech 4] right action 5] right way of life 6] right motivation 7] right awareness and 8] right meditation

Furthermore, we are taught to understand that while living correctly is not an easy pathway and that self-discovery can be very challenging and difficult it will lead us beyond the World of *Learning* onto the World of *Realization*, which in turn will lead us to our *Bodhisattva* nature and finally to the achievement of *Buddhahood*, while understanding that all form and achievement is temporary and ever changing.

"Faith is the priceless sword that will cut through fundamental ignorance." ND

NOW, *3,000 In One Momentary Life Force*
~~~ *Ichinen Sanzen*

The concept and actuality of *Ichinen Sanzen* [Ichinen = One Mind] [Sanzen = manifestation of life force and environment] tells us where our thoughts come from. Explains why history often repeats itself. It explains why humans have the cycles of life they do and why persons can be healthy for years and at other times sick, sometime poor and other times rich. **Ichinen Sanzen** explains why some countries suffer more than others, why some communities are more giving than others. It explains why some corporations are built on greed, while others have a desire to create a wealth of knowledge and science. The actuality of *Ichinen Sanzen* explains how our universe works, and how the Ten Factors and Ten Worlds of life within energizes and supports us.

So, where does thought come from? There is at any one moment many thousands of flashes of electromagnetic energy that crosses the brain, energy fields from the scientific light of awareness, buddha suchness, or ku. As this energy flashes across the brain we reach in and through our mental powers select the *awareness* that makes for realized thought.

Ichinen Sanzen [three thousand realms in a single moment of life] is the principle formulated by the Great Chinese Scholar, Teacher and Priest *Tien Tai Chi'I*. He became *enlightened* to this truth partially from within the Second Chapter of the *Lotus Sutra* in the Ten Factors or Way of the universe and saw their hidden meaning of *"mutual possession"*, as stated in the tenth factor "consistency" from beginning to end.

In the seventh chapter of the fifth volume of his work *Maka Shikan*, T'ien-Tai taught us how to see the true nature of life. *"Each moment of life is endowed with Ten Worlds. At the same time, each of the Ten Worlds is endowed with all the others, so that an entity of life actually possesses one hundred worlds. Each of these worlds in turn possesses thirty realms, which means that in the one hundred worlds there are three thousand realms. The three thousand realms of existence are all possessed by a single entity of life. If there is no life, that is the end of the matter. But, if there is the slightest bit of life, it contains all the three thousand realms."*

As we have been sharing, life is eternal and All is a part of the Oneness of universal energy and light, life itself. *Eternal Life is simply the moment of NOW.* Tien Tai Chi'I realized that the world evolves around these *Ten Factors* as expressed in the *Lotus Sutra: 1] form 2] nature 3] substance 4] power 5] function 6] cause 7] relation 8] effect 9] result* and *10] consistency from beginning to end*. These are qualified by the *Ten Worlds* and the The Realms of Existence. *1] hell 2] hunger 3] animality 4] anger 5] humanity 6] heaven 7] learning 8] realization 9] bodhisattva 10] Buddhahood.*

Three Realms of Existence: 1] the realm of the five components of life: form, perception, conception, volition and consciousness, 2] the realm of living Beings, and 3] the realm of the environment. This is an expression of the depth of all life and the Oneness within our Universe. The Aspects of Life in turn are qualified by *Three Sets of Circumstances:* 1] circumstances related to the physical nature of manifestations of life; 2] those caused by the individual differences among the manifestations of life; 3] those caused by the nature of the place in which the manifestation occurs.

One World possessing the seed of the other nine makes One Hundred Realms. The Ten Factors that predominate All phenomena, means one hundred realms, times, one hundred factors makes for One thousand aspects of phenomena, energy or Awareness, this Mutual possession contained within the existence of the three realms of existence, equal three thousand potential realities. Any one factor may take place to be present simultaneously within a single instant of universal life sharing in the fusion of the person and the universal Law; humanity, the sun, moon, planets and stars all interconnected.

Ten Worlds, 100 Realms Ten Factors, One Thousand Aspects in MUTUAL POSSESSION of 3,000 potential Existence's

10 X 10 = 100 X 10 = 1,000 X 3 = 3,000

Every life moment possesses the potential of three thousand different realities and each life moment is *dynamically interrelated within a harmonious NOW.* Nothing is fixed and isolated from each other, All are connected. The quote: *"life at each moment is endowed with the Ten Worlds"* means that the potential for all ten conditions are present, the question is which one will we manifest, based on our physical, mental and spiritual health at this moment, under this moments conditions and circumstances.

The *Maka Shikan* further goes on to explain: *"the mind is all phenomena and all phenomena are the mind,"* the relationship between "mind" and "manifestation" is very deep and profound, in fact it is known as *"the region of the unfathomable."* We are talking here of "two but not two," the environment and the Beings are One, neither can be independent of the other. The interrelationship between phenomena and mind is obscure, hidden, deep and profound. It takes a leap of faith to Realize everything is interconnected a particle of All phenomena.

In this introduction to *Ichinen Sanzen* we have the principle of *Three Thousand Realities"* which merges the principles of the Ten Worlds, their mutual possession, the Ten Factors, and the Three Realms, all of which are given to us within the living philosophy of the Buddha Dharma, and significantly in the scientific study of Quantum Physics of today.

By bringing forth our Buddha nature we can realize the *Four Noble Truths:* 1] all existence has suffering, 2] all suffering is caused by earthly desires 3] the elimination of unbalanced desire leads to peaceful means. This peaceful means resulting in the ability to manifest the *Eightfold Path*: 1] right views 2] right thinking 3] right speech 4] right action, 5] right way of life, 6] right endeavour, 7] right mindfulness, 8] right meditation.

The point to be made here is as human beings we are made up of physical, mental and spiritual health, with an understanding of how the universe works we are given the ability to change our negative life tendencies and ever changing life conditions towards inner health and happiness.

This leads to the higher worlds of Bodhisattva, to our compassionate, empathetic, giving nature and to Buddhahood *just as we are.* We will become enlightened to All life and its environment so that when we pass into the void of what we call death, the light of *Nirvana* will BE, dispelling the darkness and cycles of life and death.

"Only the Tendai doctrine of Ichinen Sanzen is the path to Buddhahood. Even in the case of this doctrine of Ichinen Sanzen, we do not possess the kind of wisdom and understanding to comprehend it fully. Nevertheless, among all the sutras preached by the Buddha during his lifetime, the Lotus Sutra alone contains this jewel which is the doctrine of Ichinen Sanzen." ND

Tien Tai Chi'I's   Principle of NOW
Ichinen Sanzen ~~~ 3,000 in 1 Instant of NOW

Ten Life Conditions in constant motion ➔➔➔
Mutual Possession interdependent reality ➔➔➔
Ten Factors of all phenomena ➔➔➔
3 Realms Of Existence

1. Pain of Hell		1. Appearance	Five*
2. Hunger	Each and every	2. Nature	Components
3. Anger	world containing	3. Entity	
4. Animality	particles of the other	4. Power	
5. Humanity		5. Influence	Humanity
6. Earthly Heaven	Today's	6. Internal Cause	
7. Learning	Quantum	7. Relation	Environment
8. Bliss Realization	Physics	8. Latent Effect	
9. Bodhisattva		9. Manifest Effect	
10. Buddhahood		10. Consistency from beginning to end	

* Five Components: Form, Perception, Conception,
Will Power, Consciousness

➔➔➔   10 x 10 = 100   ➔➔➔   10 x 100
= 1,000   ➔➔➔ 1,000 x 3 = 3,000

Where Do Our Thoughts Come From ?

Our thoughts come from the energy of the Five Components. Our will power chooses which of the 1 in 3,000 potential realities take place in our brain in any one millisecond. Through our will power we select that which we choose as thought or let it pass simply as energy and potential messengers of seeing, listening, stress, sleep, anger, love, joy, bliss. The power of the mind uses the same phenomena of energy that makes up of our universe!

The Moment of NOW !

Summary of Fourth Sharing Session

We have learned and shared that Everyone, not just scientists and academics, can come to understand how the world and our universe evolves and works in One's everyday life. One starts with an understanding of the Law of Cause and Effect, realizing that there are Ten Factors that make up the way the universe unfolds.

Within the Ten Factors, are the Ten Worlds within the Dharma Wheel of constant change. As the stars and planets come to life and die all are affected by the *mutual possession* of the principle of *Ichinen Sanzen* or *momentary life force* within the Three Realms of Existence.

These in turn are qualified by the three sets of circumstances and the Twelve Factors within the Law of Causation. Accordingly every life moment possesses three thousand different instant possibilities or potential realities, right NOW!

Through an understanding of the Ten Worlds, the Ten Factors, the principle of *Ichinen Sanzen* and the Twelve Linked Causation, we have the answers and tools to lead a wonderful dynamic life of health and happiness.

"In our understanding of the moment of NOW, Ichinen Sanzen, the absolute meaning of the workings of eternity, we truly find the absolute freedom to attain Buddhahood." HL

Discovering Your Buddha Nature

NAM~MYOHO~RENGE~KYO

The Buddha - The Law - The Beings

Sharing Session   FIVE OF SEVEN

1] Health, The Trinity of Body, Mind & Spirit
2] KARMA ~ The Vast Subject
3] Curing Karmic Disease
4] Repaying Debts of Gratitude & Good Fortune

Health is a *fusion* of *objective reality* [i.e. I am sick, I am healthy] with *subjective wisdom,* [i.e. I will heal myself, I will give daily thanksgiving.] This is the Oneness of our Person with the infinite eternal Law of Health. The Buddha of absolute freedom is simply one of "No Doubt," Living in the World of Humanity, having for the most part left the worlds of Hell, Anger and Animality behind, we empower our true self onto the higher Worlds of Heaven, Learning, Realization, that way we may enjoy perfect health most of the time, prosperity in mind and spirit.

HEALTH Body, Mind & Spirit, the Elements of Earth, Wind, Fire, Water

1] Health is the most important self-empowering life force

2] Disease is dis-ease and One can Heal most illness of body, mind and spirit

3] We can transform our sickness and suffering, into health, non doubt, and wisdom

4] We can surpass even indefinite karma and transform sickness into wellness

The greatest disease on earth is not cancer, hunger, old age or suffering. It is DOUBT. Doubt blocks the way to wisdom, understanding and richness of being. Doubt is the pathway to unbalanced fears, negative karma and suffering. Non-doubt leads to the three virtues of personal freedom, maturity and enlightenment in this lifetime.

When health is understood as a *Three Part Oneness* then a correct balance is achieved in giving One vitality and excellence of health. The balance of the physical, mental and spiritual are much out of order for masses of individuals. This is why billions of dollars are made by marketing fad diets, by the sale of pharmaceutical drugs and by a western culture of dependency on doctors and sick care, instead of wellness and health care.

Looking at the balance of one's spiritual nature in co-ordination with one's physical nature we easily see much mental affliction. Separation of the spirit and the physical is impossible; yet too many deny that they are connected and herein lies a major cause of cancer, depression, doubt and mental illness.

What is it that holds people back from the realization that we are spiritual beings on a human journey, not human beings on an earth journey? Taking care of our physical, mental and spiritual health is a daily issue we are responsible for. It takes work to be healthy. It takes courage to research the religions of the world and come realize One's Buddha-nature. The world is filled with religious falsehoods. This is one of the reasons why Nature fights back producing both individual, community and world wide environmental karmic retribution.

For too many the aspects of our lower animal nature seem easier to live in, than to seek self empowerment through discipline, effort and realization. Still, we see many cases of so called miracles in humans as they awaken in a time of great stress, sickness or disease, as they fight back and heal themselves that they might live another day, year, or two. Getting connected to the miracle of Spiritual Health, there is much proof that a positive attitude and energy is far more powerful than doubt, and concentration on negative sickness.

For those with an active living philosophy of Health, the Way of the Buddha Dharma is one of living in harmony with Ones environmental energy. Perfect health means understanding the *vital life force* of both the inner and outer self. This is the eternal balance between the physical, mental and spiritual nature within One's life.

Three Properties of Health

1] property of communication with the infinite eternal Law
~ Spiritual Health

2] property of maturity and wisdom
~ Mental Health

3] property of action for a healthy body
~ Physical Health

In this Introduction to the living philosophy of Buddha Dharma we have noted that faith, practice and study enable all of us to change out personal challenges into wisdom, to turn poison of the body and mind into the medicine of health and happiness.

According to the *Three Proofs,* Documentary, Theoretical and Actual we are given the method of achievement. Documentary Proof says: "the chanting of the *getha* or mantra the all inclusive title of the complete teaching of the *Lotus Sutra*, is a practice that involves both body and mind and it's benefits likewise appear in both material and spiritual aspects of One's life. *Nichiren* shares with us it is like the roar of a lion, so what sickness can therefore be an obstacle?"

As we have shared over and over in these sharing sessions *the Five in One Meditation, breath, visualization, sound, awareness and spiritual contemplation* affects all three forms of Health: physical, mental and spiritual. One breaths, sees, hears, becomes aware and reaches joyous contemplation. Our physical form indicates that which we see outwardly: color, form, texture, body and so on. Our spiritual form is that inner and invisible form most cannot see or recognize. The Buddhist philosophy then is "two, but not two," yet very few can fathom that the two are One.

Matter and Spirit are two distinct classes of reality, but are One in their fundamental entity. The Oneness of the Body and Mind is the Spiritual entity we are as human Beings.

From the perspective of the *Oneness of the Person and the Environment* we tend to see the world as divided into two, that which effects our self and that which is outside our self. We are the living subject and we have an objective environment. Again we see the aspect of "two, but not two." The energy force in the air around us, cold or warm, sunshine or rain, can affect our emotions and behaviour, exerts an undeniable impact on the social and environmental nearness which surrounds us. Think for a moment of being in a hospital ward, stuck in a bed and having a serious disease. Now think of a country cottage with a vast field of wild flowers and a creek running through to the tall trees and a full bright moon. Which dimension fills you with greater peace? A person whose life tendency is that of Doubt will bring forth anguish, stress and sickness. Those with an absolute positive nature will enjoy the sunshine, regardless of the weather.

Earlier in our studies we had an introduction to the Law of *Cause and Effect.* We make causes at each moment of life, through our thoughts, words and actions. Sickness then, whether serious or light, can be looked on as an Opportunity to reflect on our being and to work on change within, so that the oneness of body and mind may find perfect health. Here we have here a *Master Key* to transforming health into peaceful means.

It is a great Human Revolution, when just one person decides to achieve the state of health with no doubt. This is not an idealistic feeling, but is firmly grounded in the Buddhist principle of the Oneness of Life and the Environment. We have the power to change poison [sickness] into medicine [health].

Theoretical Proof with regard to Health states, "if an illness cannot be cured, it is the result of definite karma. But if the illness is derived from indefinite karma, it can be cured." It also says, "sincerity can eradicate even definite karma, to say nothing of karma, which is indefinite." ND For example, a man who is born blind, cannot acquire his eyesight in this lifetime. This lack of normal sight belongs to the karmic retribution as a result of definite karma from past lifetimes. On the other hand ordinary illnesses belong to the karmic retribution as caused by indefinite karma.

Bad health karma can be changed by listening to right motivated health care doctors and specialists, by scientific technologies, by our personal efforts and by daily conscious contact with the universal Law via sound Meditation by a balance of the physical, mental and spiritual aspects of One's health.

Actual proof, means a tangible result from an action taken. This proof is something you can point to and say, I see a difference, I see something I didn't see before. It shows a benefit, a positive result that helps empower one's wisdom and Buddha nature.

When it comes to health we shouldn't take it for granted. When it comes to life and death, we should remember, " we are pulled from the womb, we inhale, breath and begin our individual life." Yet we know, "life is temporary. One exhales his or her last breath with no hope to draw another. Not even dew borne by the wind suffices to describe this transience. No-one wise or foolish, young or old, can escape death. One should learn what is needed to prepare for the last earthly moment and give all else second priority." Myoho-ama Gozen

---

"A truly wise man/woman will not be carried away by any of the eight winds: prosperity, decline, disgrace, honor, praise, censure, suffering and pleasure. Neither elated by prosperity nor grieved by decline. The heavenly gods will surely protect one who does not bend before the eight winds." Asvaghosa

---

KARMA ~ *The Vast Subject*

The idea of Karma goes back over 6,000 years to the Egyptians, appearing again in ancient India some 2,300 years ago. As Buddhists we know: "It's aim is guidance, It's methods are instructive, It's functions are redeeming." The word *"karma"* comes from Sanskrit and means "action" or "deed." Those seeking a life philosophy come to understand that we can and indeed must learn to take responsibility for our own *"actions"* in this life. The fundamental concept of karma is that we are responsible for our personal actions and free will. We come to realize it is not fate or luck, or some supernatural power that shapes our lives and destiny. Rather we come to appreciate that it is our own actions made up of our own thoughts, words, and deeds that produces life's challenges and blessings. It is ownership of life, this is *My* "KARMA"

Even our smallest negative energy impulse produces an effect, just as the smallest of sparks can set off a great forest fire. Each of us is made up of billions of soul particles, the manifestation of cellular matter, that we consciously or unconsciously interplay within the *Ten Worlds* and *Ten Factors* of the Infinite Eternal Law as we make choices each and every day. Again we are reminded it is important for us to understand that the "I" or "me" is not dual in nature, but rather we live within a multiplicity, a body with billions of cells and living entities within. All things including karma do not exist as an independent individual person, entity or ego, all phenomena including humans exist within the karmic bonds of our vast energy producing universe. We are part of a larger whole, we co-exist with one another, at times influencing each other positively and at other times negatively. When we study history we get the picture. It is a fundamental principle of the Buddhist teachings that a cause will, without fail, bring about an effect.

The manifestations of the various karmic causes and effects in life are controlled within the Dharma Wheel of the *Ten Worlds*. Sometimes we are happy sometimes sad with constant variations that we select over our days, months and years. The innumerable forms of joy and suffering present waves in the ocean of our life that surge and fall. Faith helps us to weather the sea of suffering and help us cross to the shore of real happiness. Dynamically through our positive *Spiritual Health* we create *Karma* that bring wisdom and enlightenment.

Make Up of KARMA

Karma is made up of Energy, Mind, Reason, Judgement, Insight and Intuition. The degree of karma one forms depends upon the strength of One's intention. The force of karma stored within each of us is always there. Whenever we encounter the proper stimulus, its effect will appear as an emotion such as anger, fear, depression, tiredness, energy, happiness, joy. Karma is eternal, it is the energy of action that brought us here, it is in our everyday life and it is the deep energy matter in future existences.

This is why we should always seek out environments which have a good influence on us. All around us today we see the effects of negative news, false knowledge, too much information causing much confusion in the daily rush of life. We all know highly stressed people, friends and loved ones who encounter negative external influences in their relationships, careers or other life challenges. Because we all are born into this *saha* world of endurance, we should acknowledge that through our collective karma we can fall under negative influences, which will lead to our unhappiness. This is why it can be difficult to believe that we can truly build a place in the living philosophy of the Buddha Dharma known as the *path beyond backsliding,* living a pure and indestructible life force. We find this pathway through faith, practice and study. Changing our negative karma into positive karma, through building a lifestyle of health, happiness and riches.

Types of KARMA

Let's briefly consider some of the types and degrees of karma from the Buddhist concept. Karma can be broadly divided into positive karma and negative karma. Good karma arises from positive mental functions such as patience, empathy, compassion and love, while evil karma stems from negative mental functions like self will, pride, greed, lust, fear or anger. When we are born we bring with us karma from our past which has accumulated in the depths of our many lives. This answers many of our questions about why some people seem born "lucky" or with so much good fortune while others are struck with serious diseases.

We are told there are many kinds of karma. In the Gosho "On Prolonged Life" *"Karma may be divided into two categories: mutable and immutable"* and we are further told that we may change our karma, *"sincere meditation will eradicate even immutable karma, to say nothing of karma which is mutable."* Immutable karma will always produce a fixed result, while the effect of mutable karma is not absolutely fixed. It is generally considered that heavy causes, whether good or evil, produce fixed or immutable karma, while lighter causes create mutable karma. In the Buddha Dharma of *Nichiren Daishonin* we learn how to change all forms of karma, through faith, practice and study. In the *Fugen Sutra* we read that *"the sea of all karmic obstacles arises from illusions. If you wish to make amends (for some past karma) sit upright and meditate on the true entity of life, and all your offences will vanish like frost and dewdrops in the sunlight of enlightened wisdom."* This is rather heartening and hopeful, giving us the opportunity to expiate negative karma and produce positive karma.

There is much to know and worlds beyond knowing, beyond human word forms. So, my meditation for you is to accept your karma, give thanks for it, for you have earned it. If you are not happy with your lot in life, you now have a *Treasure Jewel*, the great gift of your Buddha Nature to accept life's challenges and change negative karma into positive karma, into a life-force of indestructible health and happiness. Congratulations on reaching for your inner most self!

Curing Karmic Disease   Our Negative Karma

We have a right and an ability through faith to challenge our karma, bringing forth our inherent Buddha wisdom and enlightenment. The Buddha philosophy holds that one born into the world of humanity has a life cycle of between 120 to 130 years. Within this cycle some are born with the karma of longevity while others come to earth with the karma to die young. While too many people never discover the Joy of living, living lives of dependency, depression, loneliness and a multitude of sickness. This is not the way to happiness and freedom.

Through these sharing sessions we are receiving the benefits of *Discovering Our Buddha Nature.* We have been given the gift of the Buddha's highest teachings and have learned the Five in One sound meditation [breath, visualization, sound, awareness, spiritual contemplation] chanting of **Nam~Myoho~Renge~Kyo,** the all inclusive title of the *Lotus Sutra, w*hich carries with it the energies of the entire Buddhist teachings.

The buddha of absolute freedom brings the promise that everyone can affect their karma, regardless of economics, country or culture. When we experience sickness or disease let us not think that it is cause for grief, but rather as opportunity to learn from our experience and heal from within.

Let us ask the question; "where is the power of the Buddha we receive through sickness?" In asking this question we can then ask what are the *Six Causes of Illness*?

The *Maka Shikan* sutra says they are:

1) Disharmony of the four elements, (earth, wind, fire, and water)
2) Immoderate eating or drinking
3) Poor posture and not enough exercise
4) An attack by demons from without,
5) The work of devils from within,
6) The effect's of one's karma.

Naturally, the question arises in our minds, what do we mean by demons and devils? In the Buddha teachings we come to understand "demons" and "devils" to mean harmful influences from the environment. Pathogenic bacteria might be an example. Negative internal workings of the mind are another example.

So a time of personal illness can be recognized for what it is, an opportunity to dissipate sickness. It is an opportunity to *change poison into medicine.* Let us understand and accept that All "dis-ease" has a spiritual nature, then we can utilize the eternal powers of *"Myo" [mystic energy]* to heal. We are told that the most difficult diseases to cure are those from the effects of negative karma. The *Maka Shikan* further states that, "illness occurs when evil karma is about to be dissipated." So we can truly appreciate that through disease we have a pathway to healing. We are offered the opportunity to expiate our karma in this lifetime. *Nichiren Daishonin* tells us; "What joy is ours to expiate in one lifetime our slanders from the eternal past." This positive statement comes from a compassionate Sage who suffered exile, many persecutions and even attempts on his life. Let us challenge our karma by remembering that shallow difficulties are easy to embrace, but the profound are difficult. We must take courage and take on even the most difficult of life's problems with a brave heart, so that we may expiate our karma, find peace, serenity, wisdom and enlightenment in this lifetime.

Three Ways To Overcome Obstacles & Sickness

In the Light of the Buddha teachings, Faith enables us to:

1] purge ourselves of negative past and present karma
2] lead One to "No Doubt" that all sufferings can inevitably lead to happiness
3] remember that without life's difficulties we would have no way of showing practical proof, no way of seeing, feeling, showing faith working in our lives.

Repaying Our Debts of Gratitude & Good Fortune

Life is filled with many mysteries of family, relationships, career, health and economics. Yet, how often do we forget it is our challenges that help us to know the difference between suffering and happiness? We must awaken to our responsibility and the importance of looking into life's difficulties and opportunities, finding acceptance of all of life's mysteries and give thanks for all of them. Our Health is dependent on the acknowledgement and the repaying of our debts of gratitude.

Four Debts of Gratitude

We are told that the four debts of gratitude include:

1] Debt of gratitude to our parents for life and what they give us
2] Debt of gratitude to our governments for the benefits they provide
3]Debt of gratitude to all living beings that come into our life
4] Debt of gratitude for the Three Treasures

Buddhists have much good fortune! By meditating each and everyday they are granted for the most part, the gifts of patience, understanding, and mindfullness. This gift brings calmness and joy in equal manner. As we have shared earlier, science has now proven what the Buddha taught 2,600 years ago, that "sound meditation" or chanting makes physical changes within the brain that counter-balance fear, anxiety, anger and other lower world manifestations including the inability to show gratitude for life and its challenges.

1] Whether our *Parents* loved us or hated us, they gave us life. From their ability or inability to be good parents they give us lessons from our very first breath of life. How we accept and handle what our parents gave us is in our ball park. What the Buddha says is profound, we pick our parents from our past

existence and come into being in this lifetime by virtue of past karma. Therefore, we must be grateful and give thanks in every way for our parents. For example lets say we did not have good parents. As Buddhist's it is very important that we meditate and pray for their enlightenment, that we forgive their ignorance and inability to be good parents. How much more so then should we want to give our blessings to good parents? When was the last time you said a prayer of thanksgiving for the two Beings who delivered you into this world?

2] In former times most of the population were subservient to their Lords or Sovereigns and life could be ended quickly if One got up on the wrong side of the bed, if you know what I mean. Today most of us have a totally different kind of freedom. Yet seldom do we take the time to meditate and pray that those elected to power, those who make the decisions regarding *Government* regulation and taxes, be granted Right Thinking and Right Motivation so they can make Right Decisions. How often do we take an active role in what we think is right for our government to be doing? From a Buddhist perspective we are empowered spiritually to make offerings to those in power who make decisions that affect our lives and so we should. One of *Nichiren's* most profound energies in his attempt to pay his debt of gratitude for life was called the *Rissho Ankoku Ron*, during the reign of Emperor Kameyama [1249 -1305] in his desire to share with the government how peace could come to the government and the land.

3] Next, lets understand what the Buddha means when he says we owe a debt of gratitude to all *Beings* who come into our lives. With over six and a half billion people on earth we get to touch base or meet only a few indeed. We don't normally think of it this way. We think in our ego personalities that we know a lot of people. In fact, in our lifetime we may meet between 5,000 and 10,000 people depending on our career and the lifestyle we live. Of the people we meet perhaps we will get to know 500 from a little to very well. Besides family, of these, perhaps 50 will become close friends.

From a Buddhist perspective then *every* human we meet is important and has a role to play in our lives. All beings that we meet are potential soul-mates. They are someone we have met before in another form time or space, or someone new to us in our current world.

From a Buddhist perspective all people who come to teach us lessons, challenge our personality, give us gifts, love or to despise us each person has a role to play in our life. Our opportunity is to see beyond the hurt or happiness and enabling One to be wise enough to expiate negative karma and meditate for all people we encounter on our journey through life.

In all cases our debt of gratitude is easily met. How? Simply by utilizing the chanting of *Nam~Myoho~Renge~Kyo* our conscious communication with the universe, in a most profound and far reaching communication and meditation. One meditates always that the people in One's life awaken to their Buddha Nature and become wise to the true aspect of their life. Finally, we join our hands and chant *Nam~Myoho ~Renge~Kyo*, in respect to their *spiritual nature*, because they are a person we met, compared to the six and a half billion we will never meet.

4] The Three Treasures **The Law, The Buddha, The Beings**

When it comes to paying debts of gratitude to the Three Treasures we are instantly reminded that the Buddha Dharma is about "actual proof." From a Buddhist perspective life is to be lived actively with thanksgiving for the people in our life. Buddhists realize that we are not alone, everything and everyone is interconnected. All is One, a part of past, present and future within the Infinite Law of Eternity and by the connection to the Buddha, to our fellow humankind and to our environment. We owe a debt of gratitude to the eternal eternal Universal Law that governs all phenomena. We owe a debt of gratitude to the Buddha for sharing his enlightenment, sharing with the world how we can discover our Buddha nature, seek wisdom and enlightenment in this lifetime.

We are reminded in the *Lotus Sutra* that we owe a deep debt of gratitude to all our mentors and guide teachers and especially to the Priesthood who have carried the Heritage of the Law forward for thousands of years.

The Buddha, The Law, The Priesthood are the Three Treasures, The Buddha, The Law, The Sangha are the Three Treasures, The Buddha, The Law, The Beings who follow the Buddha way are the Three Treasures.

The Buddhist concept of *itai doshin,* many in body, one in mind, is how community cultural and world peace will be achieved. As we chant *Nam~Myoho~Renge~Kyo* each day as a method of paying our *Four Debts of Gratitude*; as we understand that the Three Treasures are not separate links, but rather Three-In-One within our Being, spiritual sustain-ability or *Kosen Rufu* peaceful means will be achieved. By constantly repaying our debts of gratitude, good fortune and joy will be ours constantly.

"No sickness, challenge, difficulty or problem is too great! In the seventh volume of the Lotus Sutra, the sutra of universal wisdom; we learn that this sutra is beneficial medicine for the illnesses of all humankind."
Curing Karmic Disease, ND 1275

Summary of Fifth Sharing Session

With this sharing we have seen the value of excellent Health and a manner in which to attain excellent Body, Mind and Spirit. This is not an easy matter for the billions of humans who have never heard of the eternal, infinite, universal, Buddhist Law.

With the spread of the Buddha Dharma, it is believed that health care bills would be cut dramatically if people followed the principles we have shared in these sharing sessions. However, too many people are still at the entry level in our World of Humanity. They are slow to learn, lacking in wisdom, living lives of busyness, half truths, listening to the noise, volumes of misinformation, living with mental afflictions, not able to discover their true nature, living in to much busyiness, denial, dependency and negativity.

Ask the average person on the street about Karma and they may know it as a word. Ask them about the Law of Cause and Effect and they have never heard of it. Worst yet, people buy into the falsehood that they are sinners. Not understanding that they are masters of their own body, mind and soul and that heavy karma can be changed from negative to a positive vibrational energy force.

In the introduction to Karma we shared the Three Properties of Health, and the Three Ways to overcome obstacles and sickness. We learned the make up of *Karma* and how to cure negative karma, by producing positive karma, leading to the Three Freedoms of: Health, Happiness and Wisdom.

We shared the Four Debts of Gratitude we all should be aware of, and how to pay them.

I hope you will contemplate on these matters, for they are truly profound.

> *"Much of One's Health is shaped by attitude,*
> *motivation and will power"* HL

YOUR NOTES

NAM~MYOHO~RENGE~KYO

The Buddha - The Law - The Beings

Sharing Session   SIX OF SEVEN

1] Trinity of Oneness ~ More Health
2] The Four Virtues: Eternity, Happiness, True Self, Purity
3] Meditation On the Sacred Source - GOHONZON
4] Mysteries of Birth & Death, the Transfer of Merit

Trinity of Oneness ~~~ *More Health*

The living philosophy of the Buddha teachings contains the principle of the Oneness of the Body, Mind, and Soul, the essential Oneness of the material and spiritual. The material is that which can be outwardly seen, which has the particles of colour, form, texture and so on. Our spiritual phenomena corresponds to that which is inner and invisible, such as emotion, inner personality, depression the turning of One's anger inward, reaching for joy and other positive attributes of the personality. A master key to understanding all Buddha Dharma is to realize that life is not about duality, rather moment is filled with multiplicity of choice. This expresses the fact that matter and spirit are two distinct classes of phenomena but One in their fundamental reality. The "eternal Law" of the universe always contains both physical matter and spiritual consciousness in life. Both are integral expressions of the multiplicity of the One eternal, universal Law. This is a major feature of the *Heart Sutra* on emptiness. Understanding we are not dual in nature, we are nothing and everything at the same time. The perfection of wisdom is in the realization that our consciousness, material life, volition or will power, habits, and sensations, such as mental awareness, are wonderful, but temporary, therefore empty of intrinsic existence. The energy force of all vibration moving in constant change of itself manifesting temporarily as body and mind.

Contemporary research in the fields of psychology and physiology has confirmed that the body and mind exert a reciprocal vibratory influence. Emotional stress reveals itself in physical symptoms such as ulcers or muscle tension. Physical factors, such as vitamin deficiency or a low level of blood sugar can profoundly affect One's emotional state. Deeper insight into the subtlety of this reciprocal influence has given rise to the discipline of psychosomatic medicine. While medical science has come to recognize the delicate interaction between the body and mind, it views them as "two" distinct entities. Buddha Dharma goes naturally beyond body and mind to include spiritual health. It discerns the reality of Oneness which permeates the body and mind making their physical interrelation possible.

Buddha wisdom approaches life not in terms of matter or spirit, but in terms of the reality beyond the physical, mental and spiritual health and how it manifests within each and every human. For the Buddhist there is no such thing as pure matter or pure spirit. Life is not a duality. There is a harmony of Oneness in all life in many different containers, if you will. Life invariably manifests both a physical and a spiritual aspect. This reality is forever alternating between two states, the manifestation we call "life" and the latent aspect we call "death." While we are here on earth our life exhibits earthly desire for both physical and spiritual needs. When we pass on, these functions recede into dormancy according to our individual karma. Then, when triggered by an appropriate external cause, [i.e. the void rubbing against awareness the suchness of universal energy vibration, conception occurs] our life again emerges from the dormant state and reappears in a world to once again to manifest physical, mental and spiritual properties.

We can illustrate the Oneness of body and mind with a simple analogy of a coin. A coin has two sides. Both sides have distinct features, but they cannot be separated. It is one whole coin. Matter and spirit, similarly have differing manifestations, but they are unified at the essential level of Oneness by the fact that they both manifest a quality of life within the ten directions of the universe.

What we learn from this concept is that quality of life does not exist apart from the material or spiritual phenomena of this world or from the Oneness of the eternal, universal Law. This is a very deep concept, upon which One can meditate on for a long time. In body, mind and spirit we have not two, but three, not three, but One.

It is through the daily practice of chanting *Nam~Myoho~Renge~Kyo* an act so simple, but in fact profound, that One will find an understanding of the concept of Oneness of Body and Mind-Spirit and how it affects our health and our life.

Four Virtues ~ *True Self, Happiness, Purity, Eternity*

In the *Nirvana Sutra* we find *Four Virtues* which all Beings should aspire too. In the *Lotus Sutra* in the Fifteenth Chapter we find the Four Great Bodhisattvas, Jogyo, Muhengyo, Jhyogyo and Anryugyo protectors of mother earth, they signify respectively the Four Noble Qualities of Life, True Self, Happiness, Purity and Eternity. But, how does one achieve these virtues? Would it be natural to Realize that we should start by concentrating on our present habits? What physical action or non-action are we presently doing that would block any of the four conditions? What wrongfully motivated desires do we have that would block our happiness and purity? Should we be reminded how temporary all of life is?

The *Essential* teachings contained within the *Lotus Sutra* reveals the complete and essential Four Virtues as the Buddha tells us; *"I Am here always, teaching the Law"* which is respective of the virtue of *"eternity."* *"This, my land, remains safe"* manifests the virtue of *"happiness."* *"Ever since I attained enlightenment"* the virtue of *"true self."* And the Buddha's land of *"purity and serenity"* is found in the Seventh Roll, the Twenty Third Chapter of the *Medicine King*, is in fact mother earth. *"This scripture, for the people of this land [Jambudvipa], is a good physic for their sickness."*

Within the *Lotus Sutra* we find the Theoretical proof. Theoretical proof means that a doctrine is consistent with reason and logic and does not contradict itself.

1] Eternity is the absolute, unchanging condition, which is to say everything is forever changing, nothing stays the same. The Dharma Wheel keeps turning, birth and death, beginnings and endings are eternal.

2] Happiness means different things to each of us, from a Buddhist perspective, happiness is considered a life condition free from all doubt, living in the higher Worlds of peaceful means and positive wonder.

3] True-self is the finding and manifestation of One's higher self, beyond back sliding, ego personality and delusion.

4] Purity means living a dynamic life, reflecting daily on ways to improve Oneself. Purity comes from the practice of making *"conscious communication"* with the *Infinite Eternal Law* through the Buddhist Five in One Meditation, the chanting of the all inclusive title of the Lotus Dharma Flower Sutra, *Nam~Myoho~Renge~Kyo*.

A major difference between the *Thervada* Buddhist philosophy and the *Mahayana* teachings is that complete elimination of earthly desires is not necessary, Mahayana philosophy teaches that all humankind has the ability to attain the four virtues in this present lifetime, just as we are, through faith, practice and study.

Eternity, Happiness, True Self & Purity

We must *Learn* to endure, and be filled with discipline in regards to the strengthening of the Four Virtues. To manifest dynamic forces takes time and effort, but the gifts and miracles are well worth the effort in remembering we live in a *saha* world, the world of endurance.

We are reminded by science that when iron is heated, if it is not strenuously forged, the impurities in it will not be removed. If one does not grind seed correctly, then not much oil will be processed. We are given an opportunity when others berate us or slander our person with opinion, gossip or half truths, to look deep inside, to seek the Four Virtues and find *our true self*. Within the Fourth Daily Meditation we share that we should, "pray to erase our negative karma, created by our own past causes, daily purify our faith, and practice, seeking the buddha of perfect wisdom within."

As Buddhists, we are empowered to do something about the injustice in the world around us, whether that is in the block where we live, in our community or in a country far away. We are reminded that we have been granted a true blessing in discovering our Buddha Nature. It is our responsibility then, to meditate and pray for others regardless of their beliefs, errors, suffering or pain. In this Way, we can work towards attaining the *Four Virtues* in our daily life. We can do our part to overcome the Devil of the Sixth Heaven [energy force or king of devils who dwell in the highest of the six heavens of the world of desire.] This energy force, saps the life force of all Beings. *Nichiren Daishonin* explains the Devil of the Sixth Heaven as the manifestation of fundamental darkness or negative energy.

I challenge you to understand and realize that when you chant the *Five In One Meditation* You are physically, mentally and spiritually manifesting the Four Noble Virtues of *eternity, happiness, true self* and *purity*. Each of us is a unique and special Being. Daily we need give thanks for our uniqueness and chant for the Oneness of peace within, peace in our community, and the Buddhist concept of *Kosen Rufu*. the spread of the Buddha Dharma for peaceful means on earth, that all humankind may manifest the Four Virtues.

Meditation ~ *On the Sacred Source* ~ Gohonzon

We find in the Fourteenth Chapter *A Happy Life* or *Comfortable Conduct* a statement that leads One to perhaps understand why *Nichiren* may have chosen to leave human kind with a Mandala known as the sacred source **Gohonzon**. *Shakyamuni* is sharing with the great bodhisattva *Manjusri* [*wonderfully auspicious*] and he says, "in the Latter Day of the Law [age of latter end], when they have recited, ... when they have preached, they shall be able to write....and shall make offerings to the scriptural roll, venerating it with humility and holding it in solemn esteem." The *Gohonzon* mandala, or object of Fundamental Respect, was made manifest by the Buddha of our Latter Day of the Law, *Nichiren Daishonin,* as early as 1271 c.e. and means perfectly endowed, or cluster of blessings.

Nichiren saw the need for more than statues of Shakyamuni and other Buddha's. He realized that people were becoming more educated in the 13th century, and would understand the teachings by depicting the fusion of the eternal, universal Law, the Buddha, the Protectors and all people in a written scroll of magnificent character. Both the *Therevada* and provisional *Mahayana* doctrine of the historical Buddha *Shakyamuni* have been assisting people find the pathway to their Buddha nature for almost 3,000 years. While this process of bestowing *Gohonzons* on priests, monastics and lay believers has been carried on for almost 800 years. Going back to our beginning sessions we recognize that *Nichiren* was born to give all human kind a harmonious method of practice for our current times.

Individuals who choose to receive the Precepts of the Latter Day of the Law, and take the Buddhist vows of the **Mahayana Nichiren Buddhist Sect** may receive this object worthy of great respect for personal use in their homes. For example we read the following from a letter Nichiren wrote to one of his followers on the twenty-fifth day of the eighth month of 1275 AD. *"I have received your various offerings. I am entrusting you with the Gohonzon for the protection of your young child. This Gohonzon is the heart of the Lotus Sutra and the eye of all* *the scriptures. It is like the sun and the moon in the heavens, a mighty ruler on earth, the heart in a human being, the wish-granting jewel among treasures and the foundation of a house. When one embraces this mandala, all Buddhas and gods will gather around him, accompanying him like a shadow, and protect him day and night, as warriors guard their ruler, as parents love their children, as fish rely on water, as trees and plants crave rain, or as birds depend on trees. You should trust in it with all your heart." With my deep respect. Nichiren*

From "The Real Aspect of the Gohonzon" Nichiren shares with us: *"Dwelling in the Gohonzon are all the Buddhas, bodhisattvas and great saints, as well as the eight groups of sentient beings of the two realms who appear in the first chapter of the Lotus Sutra. Illuminated by the five characters of the Eternal Law, they display the enlightened nature they inherently possess. This is the true object of worship."*

The Origin of Mandala's

The origin of the Mandala is from the ancient Sanskrit language. It means to tell a story. It is an intricate motif symbolizing the eternal, infinite, eternal, universal Law in both Hindu and Buddhist traditions. Mandalas depict various scenes, buddhas, bodhisattvas, humans and non humans. It is a guide for readers, a representation of subjective wisdom and objective wisdom and truth. It may contain honourable titles of symbolic universal messengers, and the principles of the teachings, the names of martyrs and a wide variety of other symbolic symbols of faith, practice and study. A *Gohonzon* has some forty master keys contained within its beauty and profound statement of life. Long before the 13th Century and even today a most common form of visioning the Buddha is in the form of statues. *Nichiren Daishonin* realized that statues tend to look like the vision of the culture of the country or style. This may also be a reason why Christians adopted a cross, instead of trying to portray the look of Jesus who was an Arab Hebrew. *Nichiren* in his enlightened wisdom wished all people to be enabled to attain access to the

Three Great Secret Laws. This *Gohonzon Mandala* enables One to be in touch with the universal Law, while meditating on their Buddha nature, chanting for wisdom and enlightenment.

Three Great Secret Laws ~ Method, Practice & Place

The *Gohonzon* is the gateway to our universe as the Three Great Secret Laws become One.

Method: Object of fundamental respect ~ the GOHONZON Mandala

Practice: Conscious communication with the universal Law ~ through the Five in One sound meditation chanting of *Nam~Myoho~Renge~Kyo*

Place: The place where One practices ~ One's Sanctuary of attaining wisdom and enlightenment, One's home, a Buddha Centre, or Temple

This Mandala is unlike other Mandalas. It is not round. It brings great responsibility in its gift. It is not to be destroyed or used as a fund raiser such as the Tibetan sand mandalas of impermanence. This Mandala is a vision of the eternal universe enabling the fusion of the person and the Law. How wonderful. The calligraphy of Chinese characters is elegant, sharp, bright and tells the story of the Buddha Dharma for all three times, the Former Day of the Law, the Middle Day of the Law and our current Latter Day of the Law. In addition, on the *Gohonzon* we find, *"I have respectfully transcribed this* [as a votary of the Lotus Sutra], Nichiren's Signature, and the following: *Sincerely to the people of Hokke.* This translated means to all people who believe in the words and phrases of the Lotus Sutra and the Buddha Dharma of the Latter Day of the Law. It is within the *Gohonzon* that Buddhist's go beyond Precepts, Meditation and Wisdom. Here we have an object worthy of deep respect allowing All to visit the Buddha at his place of Being.

The Mysteries of Life & Death

"When Your Dead, Your Done" Ray Charles
Of course this is only partially true but it is a heck of a statement. If we believe life is eternal, then we must believe it has more than a human beginning, and that we live within all three existence's of the past, present and future, realizing the most dynamic existence is the present moment of NOW.

"No one can escape death once he or she is born as a human being, so why do you not practice in preparation for your next life?" ND

It is important to understand that regardless of what we believe, we must not live our lives with uncertainty or doubt. From a Buddhist perspective, life has four repeated phases of existence. Birth, momentary existence up to the moment of death, death, and intermediate existence between death and rebirth. This is the living existence of *Ichinen Sanzen*, the 3,000 in 1 potential happenings we talked about earlier, living environmental eternity. Within the Nine levels of Consciousness we say there is the past, present and future, which is to say there is in reality only the moment of NOW that we get to know.

"How swiftly the days pass! It makes us realize how short are the years we have left" Nichiren

The Buddha term *consciousness* derives from the Sanskrit word *vijnana*, meaning the act of discerning, recognizing or understanding. From both a scientific and spiritual understanding we have varying levels of consciousness. The important point is the Buddha Dharma reveals the inseparability of body and mind – mind extending from the innermost realm of life to the furthest reaches of the infinite Universe, transcending our concept of time and space. The great scientist Einstein also came to this realization. At death, life merges back into the life of the cosmos much in the same way that the spray of waves dissolves back into the waters of the ocean, or the way the ocean evaporates into the universe, and air currents cause rain, which falls equally on all, finding its way again into the ocean. Our *"alaya-consciousness"* is the *eternal vital life force* that always was and always is preparing us for our next existence based on our thoughts, motivations and karmic actions in this life.

> *"During our lifetime all is recorded through our layers of karmic energy"* HL

For some, the conditions necessary for rebirth manifest quickly, while for others these karmic conditions take a long time to happen. We must be careful how we estimate time, how long is an eon of time? The *Kusha Ron Sutra* states that during the intermediate state of existence there is the power of motion, that is the interim body can freely move through space, so we should not be surprised if we "feel" the presence of a loved one who has passed away.

We must realize, it is the light and energy that reach us the individual self declining into the Eighth Level of Consciousness. In time, the personality, the body, the mind and the soul self die totally. What is eternal is only the individual Karma or accumulation of actions from our NOW eternal past. From the standpoint of Mahayana Buddha dharma, we may say that life after death exists in the state of Emptiness, *KU,* or non-substantiality, dissolving back into the great eternal universal Law flowing together with all cosmic life. Nichiren reminds us that to know who we were in a past lifetime, we only need look at who we are today. To know who we will be in the future, we need to work on our true self in this life.

From the viewpoint of life as part of a continuing co-existence with the universe death may be thought of as a period of temporary rest. Our lives have an intimate relationship to the universe as we pass through them, sometimes being born, sometime dying. Through our relationship with the universe our life continues its existence eternally through continuance of individual karma in an alternating cycle, moving about at times in a latent form and at times manifesting itself in the world of the five aggregates of consciousness, conception, volition will power, habits, sensation, mental awareness, and, material organic life or external reality. The point to understand is that electomagnetic vibrational energy is never destroyed. Life is not immortal. It simply is an eternal animating force within All phenomena.

Deceased Memorial Services

The circumstances of a deceased person's rebirth are determined by the actions performed while alive and then, after death, by the meditations offered by others in memory to his or her spirit. For Buddhists the memorial offerings often include: the sound meditation /chanting of members of family, friends and fellow Buddhists throughout various dates in celebration of the life passed, to assist during *transition*.

In the *Mahayana Nichiren Tradition*, chanting begins immediately upon notification of the death as one Buddhist passes the word along to others, who pass the word along to others so that soon the energy force of the chanting is felt by the universe from many areas of the community, country and globe. The first formal memorial service is held on the 7th day of the person's death, or as soon as is practical thereafter. The daily chanting goes on for the first 49 days, with special prayers offered every seven days on the 14th, 21st, 28th, 35th, 42nd, and 49th days. The 49th, 100th and First Annual Anniversary Days are days of special offerings, when sections of the *Lotus Sutra* are read and *Shodai* or extended chanting is done. Memory is also held on the monthly anniversary day through a *Memorial Book*.

All *Daimoku* the chanting for the deceased, is vital. The importance of chanting offering prayers for the deceased is to assist in the next rebirth, corresponding to *karmic* causality. Our meditations and prayers for the deceased are powerful. Buddhists believe this transfer of blessings effects change in the passed person's *karma* and can alter the destined circumstances for rebirth in a positive, dynamic way." No one is perfect or we can all use the blessings of others both Now and in our future existence. Also, in a practical way our meditations and prayers assist with closure on a loved One's passing.

Regarding life on this earth, the Seventeenth Volume of the *Daibibasha Ron* states, "The union of the three factors means the coming together of the father, the mother and the interim body." From the standpoint of Buddha Dharma, the life in the intermediate-existence not only chooses parents in accordance with the karma stored in its *alaya*-consciousness, but furthermore, receives from them those particular genes corresponding to its own karma. This world is a place within the vast and boundless universe where lives of freedom and good karma co-exist with unfortunate ones whose lives are stained by evil karma. A Buddhist proverb says *"more valuable than treasures in a storehouse are the treasures of the body, and the treasures of the heart are the most valuable of all."*

The fact is that we can understand the meaning of life only after we have grasped the meaning of death. If we can correctly perceive birth and death as intrinsic workings of eternal life, we can proceed from misunderstanding to understanding. From learning to realization, from realization to wisdom and to momentary enlightenment in our present form. Then each day we will be participating in the positive treasures of eternal life.

Of course this is only an introduction to the most serious subject we call death.

"Be resolved to summon forth the great Power of your faith, and chant Nam~Myoho~Renge~Kyo with the prayer that your faith will be steadfast and correct at the moment of your death. You must realize that earthly desires are enlightenment and the sufferings of life and death are nirvana." Nichiren Daishonin

Summary of Sixth Sharing Session

We learned some important lessons on the trinity of Health, including the principle that the eternal Law of our Universe always contains a mass of matter that includes particles of colour, form, texture, things that are both outward manifestations and inner ones, such as our emotions, anger, joy and other positive attributes we call Health.

We learned then that the Universal Law contains both physical matter and spiritual consciousness in life and death.

We shared Four Virtues of True Self, Happiness, Purity, and Eternal life and how One can use faith, practice and study to obtain these beautiful virtues in our life.

Then we shared the beautiful story of how the sacred source Gohonzon mandala came about and why it is so important for peace within, peace in our communities and world peace.

And we shared the Three Great Secret Laws of Method, Practice and Place, how to utilize the Buddha's teachings in our life for the here and Now of today.

Finally, we found a Buddhist perspective in the Mahayana Nichiren Tradition on the Mysteries of Life and Death. Although only a brief introduction, we learned there is nothing to fear in death and we learned the substance of our Being in our past and what we will become in our next existence.

The Buddha - The Law - The Beings

Sharing Session SEVEN OF SEVEN

1] How Do Earthly Desires Lead To Enlightenment
2] This Is The Buddhist Philosophy
3] The Buddhist Way of Empathy and Compassion
4] *Kosen Rufu* - Peaceful Means, Buddhist Practice
5] The Eternal Buddha

"This is my constant thought: how can I cause all living beings to gain entry to the Highest Way and quickly attain Buddhahood?" Chapter Sixteen, Lotus Sutra

How Do Earthly Desires Lead To Enlightenment

Nichiren Daishonin was a votary of the historical Buddha, Gautama Shakyamuni, and his highest teaching as contained within the *Lotus Sutra*. He tells us, and we can see from his life, that he was able to expiate much *karma* and for that he was eternally grateful, willing to suffer much during his lifetime on earth in the 13th century. He left over 500 actual writings and left a legacy of Buddha Dharma as guidance for the Latter Day of the Law. This includes a sharing session on *"Earthly Desires Are Enlightenment."* He tells us, "to practice only the seven characters of *Nam~Myoho ~Renge~Kyo* may appear limited, yet since this Law is the master of all the Buddhas of the three existences, the teacher of all the bodhisattvas in the Ten Directions, and the guide that enables all living beings to attain the Buddha way, its practice is incomparably profound." The *Lotus Sutra* states, *"The wisdom of the Buddhas is infinitely profound and immeasurable."*

What is meant by the wisdom of the Buddha's? It is the entity of the true aspect, or the ten factors of all phenomena, the entity that leads all beings to enlightenment. During these sharing sessions I hope you have grasped the essential meaning of all phenomena, of *Ichinen Sanzen*. This is the principle that teaches that the universe is eternal, that cosmos and galaxies are being born and dying out eternally, nature is being born and becoming extinct, humans are being born and dying. Everything is interconnected forever changing within the nature of all phenomena, not governed or controlled by some God, church or Buddhist Sect. All phenomena is forever changing within the *Ten Factors*.

In our Latter Day of the Law, *Nichiren* asks, "What then is the entity! It is nothing other than *Nam~Myoho~Renge~Kyo*," devotion to the eternal universal Law, through Buddha faith, practice and study. A commentary states that the profound principle of the true aspect is the originally inherent Universal Law. The true aspect of all phenomena indicates the two Buddha's *Shakyamuni* and *Taho*, seated together in the treasure tower in the teachings of the Lotus Sutra. *Taho*, represents all phenomena and *Shakyamuni*, the true aspect, on earth. The two Buddhas also indicate this truth as object and wisdom. *Taho* signifies the truth, as object and *Shakyamuni*, the wisdom. Although they appear as two, they are fused into the Oneness of the person and the Law, in the Buddha's enlightenment.

"These teachings are of prime importance. They mean that earthly desires are enlightenment and that the sufferings of birth and death are *Nirvana*. Even during the physical union of man and woman, when one chants *Nam~Myoho~Renge~Kyo*, then earthly desires are enlightenment and the sufferings of birth and death are nirvana. Sufferings are nirvana only when one realizes that life throughout its cycle of birth and death is neither born nor destroyed. The *Fugen* Sutra states, without cutting off earthly desires and separating themselves from the five desires, they can purify their senses and wipe away their offenses." ND

So, what does all this theological doctrine mean to us? How does it affect our understanding of the life we are living? Hopefully, it allows us to realize that all matter changes into various phenomena at various times, it is never destroyed, it is always in constant change. Life and death are One. We must *Learn* and *Realize* beyond the personality, body and mind to see the spiritual eternity. The Ice Age changed the earth in dynamic ways over time. Our time on earth is much shorter, but it is still One whole lifetime, it is your dynamic lifetime. In order to find enlightenment we must realize that we are responsible for all that happens in our life. Gossip and blame have no place in a wise person's life. Judgement of others without constant self judgement is unacceptable. We are all empowered to make a difference by being an example of patience, empathy, love and compassion. Then we can turn our earthly desires into enlightenment.

This is the Buddhist Philosophy

During these sharing sessions on the living philosophy of the Buddha Dharma we have meditated and chanted daily for each and every person who has found themselves drawn to these teachings. My daily aspiration for you is health, happiness, wisdom and enlightenment that will perhaps lead you to seek further beyond these sharing sessions opening the desire to accept the Buddhist precepts and take the Buddhist vows into your wonderful life. Peace in the world will only come about with our human revolution towards peaceful means.

As we have seen there is no beginning and no ending to eternal life. Eternity is simply this Moment! The *Ten Factors*, *Ten Worlds* and *Ichinen Sanzen* exist forever in the NOW. We have *Learned* and perhaps even *Realized* our *karmic* bond with the Oneness of All phenomena. We have come to understand that all humans have a Buddha nature and that the Buddha Way is one of compassion for self and others, of living an active life with desire, passion and wisdom.

The Buddha shares, "as to the question of where exactly hell and the Buddha exist, one sutra states that hell exists underground and another sutra say that the Buddha is in the west. However, closer examination reveals that both exist in our five foot body. We common mortals can see neither our own eyebrows, which are so close, nor heaven in the distance. Likewise we do not see that the Buddha exists in our own hearts. If one strikes at the air, his or her fist will not hurt, but when he or she hits a rock, he or she feels pain" In our introduction to the living philosophy of Buddha Dharma we have been introduced to the concept of Buddha wisdom from within the Oneness of All. We have discovered some of the Buddha's highest teachings from *Shakyamuni, Tien Tai Chi'I, Nichiren* and others. How wonderful!

In the *Former Day of the Law*, there were many blockages to individuals working on even the simplest form of schooling, education and wisdom. So, in reading the various sutras, it is important to remember the time and the age they were written. How would the teachings differ in the here and now? Even, in the *Middle Day of the Law* some 1,200 years later it was still very difficult to dedicate One's spiritual health to the Buddha-way. There were so many rules, do's and don'ts, dedications and various difficult precepts. But, as predicted in the *Lotus Sutra*, there would come a time when All could attain enlightenment in a manner conducive to the times.

In the *Middle Day of the Law*, the Great Teacher, Scholar and Priest *Tien Tai Chih'I* defined the Buddha Way through its various schools, and explained the workings of our universe. This was no small feat and in one lifetime he made a major difference in the manner of the Mahayana Traditions.

Then, in the 13 century *Nichiren Daishonin* [Sun Lotus][Great Sage], awakened Japan, and thereby the world that the *Latter Day of the Law* had begun and it was a time of the Buddha Dharma of personal enlightenment. Through One's spiritual revolution, One can find answers to all life's challenges, finding actual proof of the Buddha wisdom in One's life, leading to the desire to receive the Buddhist precepts and take the Buddhist vows. May you be so fortunate NOW!

The Buddha-way of Patience, Empathy, Love & Compassion

Few of us may be masters of any one of these four virtues, but we are all capable of attaining the enlightenment and joy that is to be found in these higher world virtues.

Patience

The state, quality, ability or fact of being patient is:

1] the will or ability to wait or endure without complaint;

2] steadiness, endurance, or perseverance in performing a task.

This implies the bearing of suffering, provocation, delay, etc. with calmness, self control and sustained courage. There are many great lessons in the *Lotus Sutra* about patience and the Buddha qualities of refraining from retaliation, of the patience of non-judgement.

Empathy

Empathy is entering into a deep understanding of the personality of another in order to understand him or her better. It is the giving of self for an others benefit! It can be love. It can be feeling the suffering of another with the desire to alleviate it.

Love

Myo [wonderful] *ho* is universal Love and our feeling of love for All existence. There are many different kinds of love - different in object, different in tendency and expression. I agree with *Pascal* who states that *the heart has its reasons which the reason does not know.* It encompasses what we see, what we hear, what we feel, what we manifest in our Being. Love is a creative force which engenders things and renews them. It is wellness of spiritual sustain-ability, health and happiness. It is a great power which draws all things together in life and death.

Compassion

Compassion is to feel pity and sorrow for the sufferings or troubles of another or others, and brings with it the urge to help. The concept of compassion, *Jihi,* originates from the idea of friend, as in a bond between equals, removing sorrow and bringing happiness to others. In compassion we find a love of giving freely from our well-life of Buddha energy.

Bakku-yoraku gives love substantial meaning. The word *bakku* means to remove the fundamental cause of suffering hidden deep in human life. This is why *listening* is so important. We can be substantially healed in just being heard! Compassion begins with empathy feeling the suffering of another as if it were one's own with the desire to alleviate it. Without this feeling of compassion there would be little willingness to help others, and there would be no practical action to remove their suffering. Compassion requires concentration, selflessness and imagination. We interpret the *bakku* of Buddhist compassion in terms of practical action.

Yoraku the second component of compassion in the Buddhist sense, means the giving of pleasure. The Buddhist term *raku* or pleasure, is by no means transient, partial, or self-sufficient, nor is it an attempt to escape from reality. Indeed, it is *the Joy of Living,* that which we call the ecstasy of life. It includes both material and spiritual pleasure. Without the deep feelings of fulfilment and the ecstasy generated by the emotions of life, pleasure in the truest sense is impossible. The Buddhist concept of this JOY involves the clean, strong pleasure that wells up from the profoundest depths of life.

What we have in these beautiful virtues is the opportunity for the *Law of Causation* to manifest in our daily living and activities bringing health and happiness.

Kosen Rufu ~ *Buddhist Perspective on Peaceful Means*

*At first there was only one person **Nichiren bo** chanting **Nam~Myoho ~Renge~Kyo**. Then there were two, and three, and so on until throughout the world millions are chanting for personal health and wisdom, daily making offerings for the Buddhist concept of "Kosen Rufu," peaceful means through Buddhist practice.*

Over these sharing sessions we have covered many topics regarding *spiritual sustain-ability*. It is significant that we have been introduced to the highest teachings of the historical Buddha *Gautama Shakyamuni*, the *Lotus Sutra*, to *Tien Tai Chi'I* and to *Nichiren Daishonin*, Buddha of our current *Latter Day of the Law*. We have found an explanation of how the mystic laws of the universe functions eternally within the Oneness of all phenomena. Through personal effort, practice and study, we become wiser and more enlightened. We can feel a difference, breathing deeper, with an enriched healthier mind, body and spirit, finding actual proof of faith in our daily life. How wonderful !

Know that our voice can help change the noisy, too busy, stressful energy of the outer world, towards one of inner positive, peaceful spiritual sustain-ability. The Oneness of everything includes the Oneness of an enlightened true-self. An energy rich calmness is happening as millions of people throughout our world desire a deeper meaning in life.

Kosen Rufu
Peaceful means beyond borders by widely declaring and spreading the Buddha-way

This is the Law of *Cause and Effect* at work through sound meditation, contemplation and peaceful being. *Kosen Rufu* is a term you may be hearing for the first time today. It is a concept that is totally in line with all our hopes and desires for a peaceful world. *Kosen Rufu* literally means to "declare and spread." It means peaceful being, without borders, and politics, acceptance of all cultures and backgrounds equally without prejudice. It means working individually and together with right motivation and action that collectively can help change our inner being and our community as well as the world, one person at a time.

We sometimes refer to *Kosen Rufu* as world peace, but it is much more. In many names the desire for *Kosen Rufu, or spiritual sustain-ability* has been with us for thousands of years. We need only look at the various spiritual communities around the world. However this is mostly in ashrams or a monastic lifestyle. They are set up to be places to get away, to find a few moments of peace, a weekend of meditation, a retreat from the busy world. How about making a small space in our home a holy place everyday? Making offerings to the universal Law, communicating between the heavens and earth just as we are. This is how *Nichiren* Mahayana Buddhists daily make offerings for peaceful means on earth with the desire for *Kosen Rufu* everywhere on beautiful mother earth.

People have hoped and meditated for harmony and peace for thousands of years, but the numbers are not nearly enough. The energy flow comes from too few and goes out in too many directions. Today, even when millions of people in many countries walk for peace, it is not enough to change the direction of those in power with their wrong motivations and lobbies of influence. We need the spiritual motivation and action of the each of us a citizens of the world participating in a practical way, offering a small part of each day towards a society and an economic cycle based on *spiritual sustain-ability* that will bring big profits and peaceful means instead of wars.

Nothing is done alone. For every action there is a reaction. This is the *Law of Cause and Effect*. Each vibration creates another vibration. Throw one pebble into a pond and notice how many circles it makes. One person can do miracles, each of us has a Buddha nature and a responsibility to work towards the goal of a healthy and happy personal life and a better world for the whole. We need to spread the Buddha's message of peaceful means so

All people can respect and accept each others cultures, religions and countries in the freedom they wish to hold. Then *Kosen Rufu* will be accomplished, as one by one, people come to see the enlightened process of the Buddha Dharma. All is One!

Kosen Rufu should not be thought of as a destiny, but rather as part of the nature of life eternally expanding. *Kosen Rufu* is not the point we arrive at, rather it is a part of the living philosophy of the Buddha Dharma expanding into society as a whole. *Nichiren* tells us in the Gosho [worthy writing] "On Practising the Buddha's Teachings" tells us, *"The time will come when all people, including those of Learning, Realization and Bodhisattva, will enter on the path to Buddhahood, and the Eternal Law will flourish throughout the land. Disasters will be driven from the land, and the people will learn the art of living long, fulfilling lives. Realize that the time will come when the truth will be revealed that both the Person and the Law are un-aging and eternal. There cannot be the slightest doubt about the sutra's [Lotus Sutra] promise of a peaceful life in this world."*

To live lives of peaceful means we must accept that we have come to earth carrying past *karma* and that it is our challenge and responsibility to *Realize* we need to change some of our character and personality traits in order to become perfectly happy. When we are clear and without doubt, then our personal light shines, our life mirror becomes bright and we have less pain, less suffering in our life and we are able to attain the highest level of health and happiness.

Ever notice how when we are in a good state of mind, others seem to notice and tell us how wonderful we look? Ever notice when we are struggling, our mind isn't clear and doubt colours our thinking? We are not quite our self? When we take the time to study and observe our "mind" we become aware of what we need to change within, then we can become worthy of respect. The task of *Kosen Rufu* is to live a practical, participating life, accepting challenge and solutions to life as part of ones *cycle of karma*, changing personal negative karma into positive karma through Right thought, Right motivation and Right action, making the world a better place to live for self and others.

Eternal Original Buddha

> Question: *"Why do Buddhas, World Honored Ones, appear in our world ?*
> Answer: *It is because they wish to cause the beings to hear of the Buddha's knowledge and insight and thus enable them to gain purity. They appear in the world because they wish to cause the Beings to understand. Buddhas, appear in the world to cause the Beings to enter into the path of the Buddha's knowledge and insight. Sariputra, this is the one great cause for which the Buddhas appear in the world."*
> Roll One ~ Chapter Two, Expedient Means, Lotus Sutra

Shakyamuni Buddha of the Former Day of the Law shares, " I have been constantly dwelling in this Saha world-sphere, preaching the Dharma, teaching and converting; also elsewhere, in a hundred thousand myriads of millions of nayutas of asamkhyeyakalpas of realms [I have been] guiding and benefitting the Beings. Good men and women! In this interval, I preached of the Buddha Torch-Bearer and others."

So, let us name a few Buddhas: Gautama Shakyamuni - historical human Buddha, Buddha of the Former Day of the Law; Dainichi - Esoteric Buddha who personifies unchanging truth; Nichiren [Sun-Lotus] Daishonin [Great Sage,] title of the Buddha of the current Latter Day of the Law; Thunder Voice Constellation Buddha; Buddha Jeweled Majestic Superior King; Buddha King Wisdom of the Pure Flower Constellation; Nento Buddha; Amida Buddha; Buddha Abundant Treasure; and Taho Buddha from a far Eastern Universe. In other words there are millions of Buddha's in all places and at all times. Furthermore, we learn: *"the place of the Buddha is the great Compassionate Heart within all living Beings."* Chapter Ten ~ Lotus Sutra

What is required is an awakening of spirit. Some 2,600 to 3,000 years ago the historical Buddha of the Former Day of the Law *Siddhartha Shakyamuni* shared that the common mortal and a Buddha are of One nature.

In our present Latter Day of the Law, the Buddha *Nichiren* provided all human kind with a practice, a method and a place of achieving great wisdom. The Buddha opens the door, but we must walk through in order to receive the benefits.

Opening the Door
A Reminder of the Three Great Opportunities for our Time

1] **Method:** The object worthy of deepest respect: the visual *Gohonzon* mandala incorporating the precepts, meditation and wisdom

2] **Practice:** A simple, yet profound method of primary practice in the Five In One Meditation, chanting the all inclusive title of the Lotus Sutra. Empowering One's life force with wonderful energy, breathing in wisdom, breathing out peace. With a secondary practice of study, growth and faith.

3] **Place:** A proper place so our life-force can be shared as an offering, felt by the *"Shoten Zenjin,* the energy forces, messengers, guardians and protectors of the infinite universal Law. Be that a Temple, a Buddha House, Your Home, a walk in the park, any place where sincere offerings are made. The best place being in front of your *Gohonzon*.

> *Buddhas are those who have completely Realized*
> *the truth of all things in the universe.*
> *Buddha, is a title meaning awakened or enlightened One.*

This enables us to hear *Nichiren* when he explains that the fundamental practice is the Five In One Meditation, the Daimoku, of ***Nam~Myoho~Renge~Kyo*** and that the secondary practice is to lead an active life-style towards achieving peace within, which leads us to the higher worlds and to Buddhahood as we are. However we are warned that knowing is not enough without practice the knowing goes nowhere. In order to achieve this higher World life-condition One must achieve the first stage: *a simple moment of faith and Realization* which *Shakyamuni* tells us is vital to understand and accept. NOW, enlightenment becomes an understanding of the real aspect of All things. The second stage is to begin to *study* the meaning of the Buddha's teachings, to have an appreciation of the reality that our buddha-nature is at One with that of the Eternal Life-Force and All phenomena.

The Chinese scholars *Miao-lo [711-782]* and *Tien Tai Chi'I* [538-597] predicted that in the Latter Day of the Law all beings would be able to achieve enlightenment and *KOSEN-RUFU* peace beyond boarders, through active buddhist practice. Understanding the profound Oneness of *Ichinen Sanzen*, the Ten Worlds and the Ten Factors, we can *Realize* the Law of Cause and Effect. In the "Opening of the Eyes" *Nichiren* shares "if we do not harbor doubt in our hearts, we will, as a matter of course, attain Buddhahood, just as *Shakymauni* taught." One's offerings of faith, practice and study develop deep faith. As one becomes clear and non-doubting about the release of negative karma, we naturally lose our illusions, doubts and sufferings, through wisdom we produce a positive, compassionate karma. Understanding the Buddha's message, sharing it with others, means many voices making offerings of spiritual sustain-ability for the growth of peaceful means. As *Shakyamuni* taught the Eternal Original Buddha and humanity are One. This helps us to *Realize* our own profound life-force and One's Buddha-nature potential. We are brought into our Being by this "life-force" the Awareness, Suchness or KU made manifest.

NOW, we realize that the Eternal Original Buddha is the great, imperishable "life-force" of the universe. The absolute, omni-present existence always causes all things to live. The Eternal Original Buddha force has been and will always be teaching and benefitting all sentient beings from the infinite past to the infinite future.

NOW, we realize the Eternal Original Buddha is not a "who", not a "man" by name, this is only an expedient means of teaching; rather the Eternal Buddha, is the same *eternal life-force that is within*. We should deeply etch these words of wisdom and enlightenment in our bodies, minds, and spirits.

Summary of Seventh Sharing Session

We shared how earthly desires lead to enlightenment! We have shared the principle that teaches that the universe is eternal, that cosmos and galaxies are being born and dying out eternally. Nature is being born and becoming extinct daily. Humans are being born and dying daily. And what we can do with this knowledge and insight.

We learned where the Buddha exists. "As to the question of where exactly Hell and the Buddha exist, one sutra states that hell exists underground and another sutra says that the Buddha is in the west. However, closer examination reveals that both exist in our five foot body."

We shared the Buddha-way of Patience, Empathy, Love and Compassion. We learned we can make a difference for Peace through our personal effort, in our neighborhood, our community, and country.

We were reminded again that the Fundamental practice is the Five In One Meditation of chanting *Nam~Myoho~Renge~Kyo*. We were reminded that the Secondary practice is to lead a daily active lifestyle towards achieving peace within, which leads us to the higher worlds and to Buddhahood as we are. We were also warned that for the average person knowing is not enough, without practice the knowing goes nowhere.

We learned the secret of where the Eternal Original Buddha manifests. NOW, we realize the Eternal Original Buddha is not a *who*, not a *man* by name, this is only an expedient means of teaching. The eternal buddha, is the same eternal life-force that is contained everywhere at all times, for humans it is found through research, contemplation and meditation, it is found within Ones self.

PART TWO

THE LOTUS BLOSSOMS

*THE SEVEN PARABLES OF THE TEACHING
OF THE FORMER DAY OF THE LAW*

Contents:
Discovering Your Buddha Nature ©
NOW Is the Time

Part TWO: Beautiful Lotus Blossoms
with *Henry Landry*, LSC, BGT

Beautiful Lotus Blossoms	135
The Lotus Contemplations	137
More Lotus Blossoms	143
Seven Parables of the Lotus Sutra	145
Re-Discovering One's Buddha Nature	153
Back to The Beginning	155
Believe:	158
Key Words	159
References & Bibliography:	161

Beautiful Lotus Blossoms

Joy In the eternal, Universal Law

Listen well and hear the Tathagata's secret and his mystic power!"

with Henry Landry, LSC, BGT,

The Lotus Contemplations

"Manjushri*, this Lotus Sutra is the secret storehouse of the Buddhas, the thus come Ones. Among the Sutras, it holds the highest place." Chapter Fourteen, Lotus Sutra

We are all gardeners! Each responsible for the seeds within our garden, be that anger, happiness, suffering or joy. From the study of the Buddha Dharma teachings of the **Former Day of the Law,** the wisdom of the **Middle Day of the Law,** or within our Realization in our current time of the **Latter Day of the Law,** we can come to understand why in all three ages the ***Lotus Sutra*** has been and is considered amongst scholars, academic and devotional lay persons, one of the worlds most important philosophical and spiritual doctrines ever written. With an open mind may these next few hours of sharing assist us in discovering our buddha-nature, as we work in our personal gardens. Faith is the seed we sow, study is the tool we use, happiness and wisdom the promise of our harvest.

Why the Lotus Sutra

So why is the *Lotus Sutra* one of the most important spiritual documents of all time? Because in Chapter Twenty Six we are promised that we will "enjoy peace and security in this life." Because of its mythical story telling principles that are very deep and profound. Because it tells us the correct Way of practice in the *fifth five hundred years* after the Buddha's passing. Because in the Lotus Sutra the Buddha makes a vow "wishing all creatures to rank equally without difference to me." Because it is all inclusive and whole in its principles, teachings and goals for humankind. Because we are reminded that the body and soul of Buddha wisdom is the food of heavenly deities, dragon kings, the energy of the sun, moon and stars, and of all humankind. Pretty good discernment.

Other examples of Sutra's include: Therevada Sutra's; the Pali Canon, the Vandana Sutra, Flower Land Sutra. Kongo Hannya Haamitsu Sutra. The Mayhayana Sutra's; Pure Land Sutra, Heart Sutra on Emptyness, Dainichi Sutra of Esoteric Buddha Dharma, and the Lotus Sutra - the one whole or complete Teaching. The *Therevada* early teachings of the Buddha are mostly contained in the Pali Cannons, and while not incorrect they only give partial answers to the Buddha's desire to end all suffering. The plain evidence of this is in fact obvious in seeing the karma in the world where *Therevada* Buddha Dharma is followed by the masses. It is important to understand that all the written teachings come from the depth of the Buddha's teachings and come at a time after his passing.

The *Mahayana* philosophy completes the Dharma Wheel of life's ever changing reality showing the Way for today with its beautiful principles and stories. Accompanying the *Lotus Sutra*, are two complimentary short teachings.

They are the *Innumerable Meanings Sutra* and The *Sutra of Meditation on the Bodhisattva of Universal Virtue*. Remembering that all teaching were Oral teaching thousands of years ago, within the teachings we witness great ceremonies of mythical proportion. In India story telling was a way to attract people to pay attention as there were no printing presses, and definitely no Internet. In these mythical exaggerations and symbolic stories we can find principles for ending all suffering. How wonderful! In the Innumerable Meanings Sutra we find a profound statement as the Buddha is about to tell the Lotus story. He is quoted as saying: *"it was with tactful power that I preached the Law variously* [because peoples personalities, desires and seeking spirit were all different] *in forty years and more, the truth has not been revealed yet."*

So what truth is the Buddha talking about? What does truth mean to a Buddhist? Does it mean, what principle should guide me to freedom? Does it mean, what Way must I follow in order to achieve health and happiness in this life and how do I prepare for the next? What about the Void, Emptyness and Ku? The master "void" can be found in the Ten Factors that run the universe of all phenomena, found in the principle of *Ichinen Sanzen*. The NOW moment of all eternal existence, as explained by *Shakyamuni* in the Former Day of the Law, and by *Tien Tai Chi'I* in the Middle Day of the Law. It is found by scientists of today in the study of *Quantum Physics*. The Emptyness is about the fullness of Life, with an understanding that the Buddha teaches there are many pathways but all pathways will eventually lead to the One Vehicle of One's Buddha or true nature. Life should be lived dynamically and fully it is not a practice run.

In the Innumerable Meanings Sutra, the Buddha warns that getting to Buddhahood is not easy. *"Men or women of the two vehicles [Learning and Realization] cannot apprehend it, and even bodhisattvas of the ten stages cannot attain it. Only a buddha together with a buddha can fathom it well."* In other words only by awakening to our true-self, our Buddha essence, will we achieve enlightenment. We are reminded that the word *buddha* simply means *awakened or enlightened*. Buddhahood is much more than an intellectual exercise or self indulgence, it is the pathway to absolute freedom.

We are told that "if a living being can hear this sutra, he or she will acquire great benefit." We are told "this sutra originally comes from the abode of all the buddhas, leaves for the aspiration of all the living to buddhahood, and stays at the place where all bodhisattvas practice." And Nichiren tells us this is in fact none other than **Nam~Myoho~Renge~Kyo!**

Understand then the place bodhisattva's practice is at home, the place where One lives and practices life. The teachings tell us to show deep respect for the time we live in and to practice the Buddhist principles of the Law, sharing it with others, bringing the teachings to everyone, through the beginnings of faith, practice and study, so that all suffering may come to an end.

The HISTORICAL LINEAGE of Gautama Shakyamuni's Teachings

The historical Buddha's teachings came about through his forty plus years of walking, talking, and orally sharing between 2,600 and 3,000 years ago in India. The time frame of his teachings is called the Buddhist Harvest as he left his enlightened teachings for all humankind. How fortunate we are to be able to practice the dynamics of the Buddha Dharma today. The messages and wisdom of the Buddha's teachings developed over the centuries by the Priesthood and many Guide Teachers is very real and like our lives came about thorough various stages and historical change while the principles remain constant.

One of the first things we realize about *Shakyamuni*, is that he chose wonderful parents. Though his mother died shortly after his birth, his mother's sister became his step-mother and we are told he grew up with many wonderful women at court, in the palace of his father. His father appears to have been quite advanced in this matter and it may have played a role in Shakyamuni being the first spiritual leader to teach women's equality. Also, his position of financial freedom and the ability to not work at a job, played a major role in his freedom to discover and then share what became known as the Buddha-way.

I speak of this in a practical manner for, as we know, in the Buddha teachings our spiritual reality comes from wisdom and with the karmic Realization of practicing in the NOW, understanding the Law of Cause and Effect.

The first group of teachings became known as *The Flower Garland Sutra* or *Kegon* teachings. It speaks to us of entering the Buddha world through meditation. This is considered a *Mahayana* Sutra and in its original form was on 81 bamboo scrolls with over 700,000 Chinese characters. It tells us everyone has a Buddha-nature. And one of it's significant teachings is the principle of *Mutual possession or Interdependent Origination of all phenomena*. Science continues to work on this even today in what is now known as *Quantum Physics*. Nichiren in the

Latter Day of the Law simplified these early teachings by giving the world the sound meditation of the all inclusive title of the Lotus Sutra.

The second grouping of the Buddha's teachings has been brought down to us as the *Pali Canon* or *Three Baskets*, also known as the *Agon* period. As the Buddha walked the earth he dealt with the day to day problems of being on the road with a group of followers and people devoting part of their daily life to their spiritual connection. The first category is mostly concerned with the code of ethics, rules and regulations of the *Sangha* or fellowship, that were to be obeyed by those who followed the Buddha around as they lived in various locations during the travels.

The second category is the "basket of threads", which consists primarily of accounts of the Buddha's life and more teachings. During this period the Buddha concentrated on sharing with people the desire to rid One-self of delusions about self and life, about cleaning Oneself of bad habits and expiating One's negative karma. The real aspect of this period of teaching was to assist with awareness of what one individual could do to make his or her world a better place to live, how to be correctly Motivated in all he or she does. This is the aspect of practical everyday manners, as one develops the wisdom to move onto the deeper concepts of their Buddha nature.

The third category, is a collection of texts in which the underlying doctrinal principles presented in the *Pitaka Sutra's* are reworked and reorganized into a systematic framework as applied to an investigation into the nature of mind and matter. These teachings are known as the *Hodo* period. This period lasted some sixteen years.

The *Fugen* epilogue to the Lotus Sutra tells us that, "the three enlightened properties of the Buddha's life arise from the *Hodo* teachings," that of leader, teacher and guide who is enlightened to the truth of all phenomena so that he can alleviate suffering. The term Hodo derives from an Indian word and was translated in China as "great vehicle."

The fourth grouping of the Buddha's teaching is known as the wisdom teachings or *Hannya* period. It is during this time that the Buddha teaches about letting go, of understanding we make our own sufferings and that nirvana means selflessness. Because of our strong consciousness of the first six senses it is very difficult to understand that our minds and bodies are only temporary and that in the big picture we do not utilize these lower senses of feeling, seeing, smelling, touching, hearing, even consciousness, except in the here and NOW. Our illusions and suffering come from not understanding the higher levels of conscious, the seventh, eighth and ninth.

The fifth group of teachings, the last eight or nine years, is called the *Dainichi* period. This is the time when the Buddha senses he will be leaving earth shortly. He is now seventy at a time when the average male lived to be around forty. He brings everything together over a period of eight years. This became the teachings of the *Lotus Sutra*.

In his final days, in his *Nirvana* talks, he shares that One's enlightenment is not found in powerful leaders or other persons but rather, from within our very selves, within our spiritual Being. *Nirvana*, like life and karma, comes in many levels of energy force, is the ending of selfish desire, illusion, and selfishness. When we die, we do not die, we return to the Eighth Level of Consciousness of eternal karma, after which becoming *Aware* we are reborn in our next existence wherever and however that may be.

For Buddhists this is very exciting, all fear of death is expiated knowing from our practice that our next existence will be one with the forces of light and energy, as we join the Buddhas of the Ten Directions awaiting our next incarnation.

More Lotus Blossoms

Nichiren suffered for many years and through several persecutions including threats to his life, the burning of his home, exile, the killing of some of his closest advisors, but nothing stopped him from proving NOW is the correct time to follow the Buddhist teachings as set out in the *Mahayana Lotus Sutra* on which he founded his new Buddha Dharma School in 1253 c.e. Today, nearly 800 years later as millions practise in countries around the world his proof is self evident.

What he discovered some 220 years into the beginning of our current *Latter Day of the Law* was that the reason for the [what history sometimes calls]Dark Ages, was because no one was listening to *Shakyamuni's* desires for peaceful means and an end to suffering in the *"fifth five hundred years after my passing."*

In the "Opening of the Eyes" by *Nichiren* we find, "All the provisional sutras such as the Kegon, Hannya and Dainichi ..... fail to make clear that the Buddha attained enlightenment countless aeons in the past.... these sutras are guilty of two errors. First, because they teach that the Ten Worlds of existence are separate from one another, they fail to move beyond the provisional doctrines and reveal the doctrine of *Ichinen Sanzen* as it is expounded in the theoretical chapters of the *Lotus Sutra*. Second, because they teach that Shakyamuni Buddha attained enlightenment for the first time in India and do not explain his true identity, they fail to reveal the fact, stressed in the essential teaching, that the Buddha attained enlightenment countless eons ago. These two great doctrines are the core of the Buddha's lifetime teachings and the very heart and marrow of all the teachings."

Nichiren continues, "during the Middle Day of the Law, One man alone, the Great Teacher *Tien Tai Ch'I*, understood and expounded the Lotus Sutra and the other sutras." In the sources of Chinese tradition of Oriental Civilizations, we find that when the Emperor Wen of the Ch'en dynasty and the Emperor Yan of the Sui, gave him an audience to establish the correctness of his views in debate with the Priests of other Sects, it was easy enough to establish the true Mahayana, from the provisional Mahayana Buddha Dharma.

We are reminded that within the Lotus Sutra and other Sutras that many Buddhas often appear to witness the teachings, but it is only in the *Lotus Sutra,* that *Taho Buddha* of the Eastern Pure Universe appears and says, *"All that you have expounded is the truth!"*

We should try to establish in our mind that in the final analysis, all phenomena are contained within our own life. Therefore, the words of the Buddha, contained in the *Lotus Sutra*, are ultimately about us. That is to say the reason Buddha's appear is to awaken our spiritual Health so we can practice in the here and NOW.

SEVEN PARABLES of the Lotus Sutra

Enlightenment comes when we master our minds, rather than letting emotions and ego driven decisions cause personal suffering in our life. HL

Beyond the joy of the daily practice of chanting the Five In One busyness of *Nam~Myoho~Renge~Kyo*, we find within the *Lotus Sutra* seven remarkable stories or parables that offer principles for us today. Part of the difficulty in any academic or theological study is how to relate the works in a manner of understanding for our everyday thinking and meditation. I hope I have succeeded in bringing the Lotus Sutra's parables into the light of today for you. My hope is that seeing here how the stories relate to us today, you will embark on the study of the actual *Lotus Sutra*. It is truly a source of inspiration within the One Vehicle manner of attaining much wisdom on the pathway to enlightenment.

1] The Burning House   Lotus Sutra Chapter Three

This tells the story of how a father upon arriving home, knows his children are at play in his rambling house that is filled with all kinds of creatures and various manner of things. Moreover, a portion of the house is burning. It is a very big house and the children playing inside to do not realize that the house is on fire. When the father dashes in to save them, they are too wrapped up in their pleasures to listen to him telling them they must get out. In order to get them to listen he promises them wonderful gifts of horse drawn carriages filled with many treasures and riches. In today's world he would be promising a *Mecedes Benz*, or a Villa by the sea. Finally the children come out to safety and the father is relieved.

The story is very graphic in detail and not easy to read, but there is a reason for this. The message of this story is people are too wrapped up in themselves, their jobs, and their pleasures. The father is the Buddha, and we are the children. The house is our society at large. It is the desire of the Buddha to awaken us to the fact that earthly desires can become enlightenment but not when we miss the spiritual responsibility that goes with One's blessings. Life is much more than competition and pleasure. Billions of humans do not Realize the Universal Law and do not relate to, the Law of Cause and Effect. Too many people live not understanding they have so much more hidden within their true nature.

Like the children in the story we need to come out of the house of busyness so that we can build true self esteem and find much more profit and peace in our life. Greed, gossip, competition and emotionally playing with peoples lives is done by those who use their strength to send out negative energy felt by our universe which greatly affects our environment and peacefulness in our world.

Once we become awakened to our Buddha nature, we can turn negative energy into positive energy, turning our doubts into riches. We must stay away from negative influences. People who emotionally drain us. We must realize we have a responsibility to reach for our personal carriages filled with many treasures and riches as we seek health and happiness for ourselves and others. We need to balance our physical, mental and spiritual Health that we may turn our earthly desires into wisdom and enlightenment.

2] Wandering Son   Lotus Sutra Chapter Four

Expressed about 800 years before the story of the lost son in the Christian bible, the stories are similar in their message. This is the story of a young man who leaves home to discover the world for himself. While just a boy he runs away and ends up wandering around working from job to job for many years. As karma would have it one day he ends up in the town where his father has settled after having searched for his son for many years. Now when the father spots him, the father knows his son immediately, but is frightened that he will run away again if he approaches him directly. So he tells a couple of his employees to go to the son and offer him a job on the estate. He accepts and over time is given more and more responsibility and the old man the owner of the estate takes him into his confidence as an advisor teaching him all the ways of the business and property management. Now the son feels that he knows this man, but he still does not realize him as his biological father. He is very grateful that the man had indeed given him back his self confidence and ability to see the effects of the good life. The father knowing the nearness of the end of this lifetime calls in a host of his friends and advisors to tell them all that indeed this is his long lost son. The astonished son learns that he will inherit all his wealth, his life changed forever.

The message in this parable is that we may wander around in busyness, doubt and longing, until we discover our true spiritual self. The father is once again the Buddha and the son is all living beings longing for a better life, but not willing to Realize their spiritual riches. The world is filled with people who do not understand that we are *energy* transformed temporarily into a body and mind to take on new lessons about our revolving lives. In the story the son is first made to do hard dirty work. The symbol here is to clear our mind of illusion. But even in clearing One's mind, One does not necessarily see the connection between One's eternal Buddha nature and One's present human nature, that takes faith.

The message in the story is that without diligence and daily personal growth One may not in this lifetime recognize their truest, most wonderful self and the ability to be rewarded by universal blessings of more riches than we can ever re-pay. This parable symbolizes that we should awaken to the worth of our true nature.

3] Parable of Herbs   Lotus Sutra Chapter Five

This story is to help us understand the relationship between the Buddha's teaching and the ability of humans to receive the blessings of wisdom and enlightenment through One's lessons of life's provision. In this parable there is a great cloud covering the sky and then there is vast rain. The great cloud is the Buddha covering all humankind. The Buddha explains to his listeners that the rain from the heavens falls equally on all things, as does the Buddha's blessings, sometimes producing weeds, sometimes producing good healthy crops. Everything bears fruit according to its unique nature. The world is filled with billions of personalities, yet the Buddha's teachings are equally available to everyone. One will be able to receive life's blessings according to where One is at in their garden of Sowing, Maturing or Harvesting.

4] The Magic City   Lotus Sutra Chapter Seven

Up until now the Lotus Sutra's early chapters are all about the Buddha and the universal Law of the Buddha Dharma. Within the Law of Cause and Effect the story telling now moves to "cause" in past relationships.

This is a story about how we do not understand the relativity of time. It is the story of a father who has sixteen sons, each of them with their own personal successes, but in hearing of their father's enlightenment stop what they are doing and bring many gifts home so that they can pay homage at the terrace of the Buddha. All the sons entreat the Buddha of Universal Wisdom to roll the Wheel of the wisdom teachings for they too wish enlightenment. The tale takes on the qualities of many, many visitors and a magic city with palaces radiant with light. Everyone is amazed for it is understood that rarely does a Buddha appear. And when he does so it is hopefully in order to teach all Beings. The party goes on for a long time as the visitors reflect on the many messages. In this story we find the Law of the Twelve Causes, the link chain of dependent origination. Then the Buddha goes into deep meditation, while the sons carry on the teaching of the Buddha Dharma. Finally in this complicated tale we awaken to the fact that the sixteenth son is in fact *Gautama Shakyamuni* who comes to earth to teach the Universal Law of enlightenment. The teaching here is that our Buddha nature is eternal, we had it in the past, re-discovering it in our present existence knowing that it will be in our future existence.

5] The Gem In the Robe
Lotus Sutra Chapter Eight

In this story we have the promise of our destiny. In this case five hundred are promised buddhahood, "as even the lowly disposed and the neglectful will gradually become buddhas." How fortunate we are to have dear and cherished friends, people we can depend on, respecting us just as we are. In this parable a good friend makes a very generous offering which the individual is not wise enough to realize and so spends many years in poverty and ignorance.

One weekend as a group is having a party all are having a good time. In fact some of the party goers sleep in rather late the next morning. The Host has to leave very early in the morning to go on a business trip, but he is filled with sympathy for the plight of his good friend who has shared he is going through a pretty rough time in his life. The Host decides that he will sew a precious gem in the man's clothing so that he can use it to get through his financial and worldly difficulties.

The man with the problems decides a geographic cure is in order and leaves town. Then one day returning to the town where his friend lives they meet on the street. The Host friend cannot believe his friend's stupidity, and says to him, "How could you be so stupid? Look at yourself! Did you not find the precious stone I planted in that dirty old jacket you are still wearing? I put it there so you could get out of your difficulties and start a new life of happiness. Reaching up into the collar lining he takes his jack-knife and cutting the precious stone loose, he says to his old friend, why should you be in want?

The lesson here is that with deep karma from our past existence, even when messengers, *Shoten Zenjin*, mentors and friends reach out to help us, we may not be paying attention because we are so deep into busyness, careers, egomania or just not listening. Even though all human beings have a Buddha nature that only awaits One's participation One may sleep through several lifetimes before One's Treasure Jewel becomes apparent. This modern day example asks; when will we "awaken" and take on the personal responsibility for self growth, living with right motivation in all that we do, building a better world for self and others, enabling us to assist in ending all suffering? When will we awaken to the gem in our robe, that which we call the gift of Life?

6] Kings Crown Jewel   Lotus Sutra Chapter Fourteen

Up until now there are two main themes within the *Lotus Sutra*. One is that all Beings have infinite possibilities, because of the infinite Universal Law that governs all phenomena including humankind. The parable here is the story of a major king who kept his country in peace in various ways.

One way the king kept peace was to give his various leaders small rewards and various gems to show he appreciated all they were doing to provide leadership. Rewarding some and not rewarding those, who did not take their responsibilities with right attitude and correct action. But everyone knew that in fact the king had a beautiful big gem he kept in his topknot which is to say his Indian crown. The Crown Jewel is *Enlightenment* which the king finally shares with those who have achieved a great victory.

Everything is mutually interdependent in its origination, therefore enlightenment is possible when humans tap into their Buddha Nature. Bliss, harmony, nirvana, and peaceful means are ours, just like they are for all Bodhisattvas in the *Ninth*

World of discovery and giving. The main message is that it is not necessary for us to go through all the austerities and many lifetimes this Buddha went through before arriving on earth. Enlightenment can be ours, just as we are, in the current Latter Day of the Law.

The lesson here is about living a happy life by overcoming One's daily challenges, showing our leadership. Everyone is born biologically to keep reaching for more, but sadly too many people do not Realize their potential for personal empowerment, leading to freedom. In this parable we find out that in discovering One's Buddha nature we will be rewarded with a true strength of character. Here is the opportunity through faith, practice and study to go beyond the World of Bodhisattva and achieve Buddhahood itself.

In the Essential teachings for our time, *Nichiren* revealed a method, a practice, and a place for All people to achieve wisdom and enlightenment NOW, in the Latter Day of the Law. How wonderful!

7] The Physicians Poisoned Children
Lotus Sutra Chapter Sixteen

The revelation in this chapter is the revelation of One's eternal life, the Buddha's eternal life. The parable of the Physician's poisoned sons makes this clear. This parable tells of a doctor who is a master of his profession. He comes home one day to find that his many sons have drunk some poison. Some of the children are not too badly affected, but some of the others may even lose their natural mental capacity. The concerned father and good doctor makes up some herbal medicines and give's them to his children. The ones not too badly affected take the medicine and become well again. However, the others will not take the medicine for they are too disillusioned. The father being very wise realizes he must do something more to shock them into taking the medicine. He gathers all the children and tells them he is getting old and must die soon, so he is going to go visit his friends of many years and say his goodbyes. He leaves the medicine and encourages them to take it. He leaves and a few days later sends home his assistant to tell the children he has indeed died. The very sick children are shocked by the message and take the medicine enabling them to become well. Hearing they have recovered the father returns home to everyone's joy.

The father and doctor again represent the Buddha. The children represent us with our various personalities, cultures, beliefs and families. The poison is One's many unbalanced earthly desires, false beliefs, delusions, and selfish motivations. The medicine is the Buddha's teachings. The Buddha tries a variety of means to help to end our suffering and be at One in absolute freedom.

[The LOTUS SUTRA can be purchased via our Website at: www.penlan.com]

Re-Discovering One's Buddha Nature

Throughout the *Lotus Sutra* the Buddha, with all the various entourages around him, and in all the story telling, explains that there are many choices and pathways in life. The question is when does One want to get on the main Freeway, in the One Vehicle to reach enlightenment. The doctrine of the real aspect of life was explained in the most important Second Chapter. In the Sixteenth Chapter we find beyond all doubt that the everlasting life force is eternal life. *Nichiren* in the Thirteenth Century reminds us that it is through faith, practice and study One finds the warmth of life that takes One beyond the World of Endurance. We are reminded that one day in this life is better than a thousand in the next, NOW is the most important moment in all Eternity.

The Buddha-way opens the door, but One must walk through it. When the Buddha was on earth walking and teaching, the desire to be near this teacher was great, as it must have been for Christ and Mohammed, but not long after his passing people started making up their own versions of the Buddha's teaching. This is why new messengers appear throughout time, as predicted in the Lotus Sutra, to bring people back to the main message.

The question becomes, how does One view and understand the historical Buddha's teachings? Can One follow the stories, verses, and parables of the *Lotus Sutra?* Does One need to understand the Buddhist Teachings of the Harvest? Can we fathom the votary of the Lotus Sutra, *Nichiren's* teachings in our present time?

Having come this far, my suggestion is to include reading a little of the Buddha Dharma every day. Find joy and understanding in the Buddha's wisdom teachings. Continue to take in the profound lessons in the first part of this book. Visit a Temple, seek out special places of peaceful means for YourSelf. Talk to the Priesthood, who have faithfully carried the Law down through the ages. *Practice Chanting daily.* Listen to your mentors and Guide Teachers until you become a teacher of the dynamic living philosophy of the Buddha yourself. Seek right motivated decisions for yourself on how best to attain wisdom and enlightenment. When we eliminate all fear and doubt from our lives, we become enabled to help everyone reach for dynamic quiet lives of greatness.

We can help those who are searching, seeking a spiritual friend or mentor, someone to assist them to *Discover their Buddha-nature*.

BACK TO THE BEGINNING

As we have shared people who share the *Buddha Dharma* believe life and the universe, from a scientific viewpoint, is made up of ever expanding and collapsing energy fields.

From a spiritual viewpoint, this is known as the law of *Cause and Effect*.

We have shared the belief that faith, practice and study are a vital part of the Buddha-way as One works toward personal wisdom and enlightenment. Buddhists understand life and death from a perspective that we are on earth to learn and realize lessons as particles of eternity in the here and Now!

When you hear a Gong, hear the sounds of chanting, or smell incense burning, it may well be Buddhist's making offerings to the sun, moon and stars. It is acceptance of today's challenges. It is taking responsibility for ones *karma*, turning doubt into belief, seeking protection from negative energy, gathering in the positive. It is a time of offering to the eternal, Universal Law for self, loved ones, friends, family, community and country. It is an offering that the Buddha-way of *"Kosen Rufu,"* peaceful means beyond borders through the spread of the Buddha's teachings may be achieved.

We have shared the simple and profound effect of the Five in One, sound meditation. The chanting that is the freeway to *conscious communication* with all nature and the eternal Law of our universe. Congratulations on pursuing your *"spiritual health."* You have discovered more of the truth about life and death than so many will ever realize on this temporary earthly journey.

In *Ichinen Sanzen* we became aware how all things are related in the flux of eternity. Through the Three Proofs and Three Stages of Benefit we come to realize the spiritual value of the Four Virtues and the Four Objects of Wisdom.

In *Re-Discovering your Buddha Nature* may you find meaning and purpose, happiness and peaceful means. May it open the freeway to faith, practice and study for you. We have shared much knowledge about the fusion of the body and mind, about life and the environment, our person and the universal Law, the mutual possession or Oneness of All

The karmic energy forces of *Shakyamuni, Tien Tai Chi'I, Nichiren Daishonin,* all the *Shoten Zenjin,* energy forces of our universe, and the Bodhisattvas of the Earth, [you and I] are truly protective of those who through simple faith, make the world a better place. We make a difference! Everyone and everything have a Buddha nature. All is One, from the smallest micro energy field to the macro, everything is interconnected. All is Eternal. Like a raindrop on the ocean of life, we are vital participants! The Buddha-way is a living philosophy that should offend no one. World peace will not happen until *Kosen Rufu* can be accomplished. Everyone does not have to become buddhists, but the principles of the Buddha Dharma is the way to peaceful means.

The Buddha teaches life as a perfect whole, integrating both the micro and the macro dimensions of life and our environment. It deals with Ones respect for life as well as the functions of our ever-changing life challenges as we move closer to death with each passing day.

Take faith. Keep listening to your inner voice and the teachings of the Buddha-way. Consider accepting the Buddha's precepts into your life. Attain peace of mind, practice living fully and be unselfish in your daily discipline of chanting of *Nam~Myoho~Renge~Kyo.* BE One who seeks wisdom and enlightenment.

Faith is a Personal Journey. What we seek is *actual proof* in our life. Then we can choose to receive the Precepts of the Latter Day of the Law, and live our human revolution through peaceful means so that personal, community and world peace can be achieved.

***Our earth is a land where
the Word-Spirit is heard and responded to
and the words are: Nam~Myoho~Renge~Kyo***

Thank You, Merci Boucoup, Dommo Arigato,

Respectfully, Henry, Buddha Ajari ~ Guide Teacher

―――――――――――――――

Believe:

That: Faith, Joy, Trust and Love, are Absolute Freedom of the Buddha-way

That: We are Spiritual Beings on a Human journey

That: the infinite, universal Law applies to all Beings

That: earthly desires can lead to wisdom and enlightenment just as we are

That: the *Lotus Sutra* is the Buddha's highest teachings as taught in the Former Day of the Law, in India, by Gautama Shakyamuni

That: in the Middle Day of the Law, the Buddha-way was defined and an understanding of how the universe works was brought forward by the Master Scholar, Teacher and Chinese Priest, Tien Tai Chi'I

That: Nichiren [sun lotus] Daishonin [great sage] of Japan, carried the message forward with a method and practice available to All Beings, thereby offering a way to peaceful means and enlightenment in our current Latter Day of the Law

That: the Buddha of absolute freedom is contained within each and everyone Now, it simply needs to be brought into One's Life with a method, a practice and a home. The method is your disciplined daily faith, practice and study. The practice as outlined in these sharing sessions and the home is found within Ones self.

"After the extinction of the Tathagata, if there be any people who hear even a single verse or a single word of the Wonderful Law Flower Sutra, and by a single thought delight in it, I also predict for them perfect enlightenment."

Roll Four, Chapter Ten, Teacher of the Law, Lotus Sutra

Key Words

Cause and Effect, Eternal Law in motion

Eternal Law, mutual possession of Ten Worlds, Ten Factors in constant change

Five In One Meditation, Nam~Myoho~Renge~Kyo

Four Objects of Wisdom, fundamental doctrine of Buddha Dharma clarifying the cause of suffering, and what can be done about it: 1] our earthly existence contains suffering   2] our suffering is caused by selfish craving and illusions, 3] we can do something about our selfishness and bring about an end to suffering 4] through Ones personal self-development and daily chanting *Nam Myoho Renge Kyo*

Gautama Shakyamuni, first historical earthly Buddha, Former Day of the Law

Gohonzon, sacred source mandala worthy of greatest respect, inscribed by Nichiren

Illusion, belief in things that are false

Karma, action

Kosen Rufu, from twenty third chapter of Lotus Sutra, peaceful means beyond borders by widely declaring and spreading of the Buddha-way

Latter day of the Law, present time of faith, practice and study

Lotus Sutra, Buddha's highest teaching, as taught in the last eight years of his life

Mahayana, great conveyance

Nichiren, Sun Lotus, buddha of the Latter Day of the Law

Nirvana, levels of release from suffering

Samadhi, bliss, balance, equilibrium beyond busy mind

Shoju, assisting people discover their Buddha nature, so they can decide for themselves the evolution of their spiritual nature

Shoshu, sho translates as a unit of measure, shu as pure

Six Elements, earth, fire, wind, water, energy, consciousness

Ten Factors, mystic universal Law in motion

Ten Worlds, the Dharma Wheel in action

Tien Tai Chi"I, Master Scholar, Teacher, Priest of the Middle Day of the Law

Three Stages of Benefit: 1] Practical Proof   2] No Doubt   3] Attaining Non-backsliding   The Way to these aspects is through Faith, Practice and Study

References & Bibliography:

Scripture of the Lotus Blossom of the Fine Dharma, Columbia University Press, Leon Hurvitz
The Columbia University Seminar in Oriental Thought and Religion with the cooperation of The Institute for Advanced Studies of World Religions, 1976

Threefold Lotus Sutra, Kosei Publishing Co., Bunno Kato, Yoshiro Tamura, Kojiro Miyasaka, 1975

A Guide To The Threefold Lotus Sutra, Kosei Publishing, Nikkyo Niwano, Hoke Kyo Chuo Koronsha, Yoshiro Tamura, 1962

Awakening of Faith, The Classic Exposition of Mahayana Buddha Dharma, Asvaghosa, 1900

The Gosho Reference, World Tribune Press, 1976

The Major Writing of Nichiren Daishonin, Volume 1 - 7, NSIC, 1979 - 1994

A Dictionary of Buddhist Terms and Concepts, NSIC, 1983

Thesis on the Whole being Contained in the One Instant of Mind, Sozai ichinen sho, Gosho Shimpen, translated by Martin Bradley, 2005

Kundalini Yoga for the West, Timeless Books, Swami Sivananda Radha, 1978

Powers, Prayers & Meditations, PenLan Publishing, Henry Landry, 1986

The Cycles of Heaven, Guy Lyon Playfair, Scott Hill, 1978

The Science of Breath, Yogi Publication Society, Yogi Ramacharaka, 1904

Concentration and Meditation, Christian Humphreys, Pelican Books, 1968

ORDERING

From Your Local Bookstore Worldwide

Direct from the Publisher: www.authorhouse.com

Through your favorite electronic bookstore such as www.amazon.com

Henry Landry, Life Skills Coach and Buddha Guide Teacher can be contacted by telephone at 250. 715. 1976, by e-Mail at: buddha@penlan.com ,

The Lotus Sutra, Other Books, Audio CD's, Meditation Benches, and Mandala Altars are also available from the Authors Website: www.penlan.com

The author can be reached by Postal Delivery at: 3437 Drinkwater Road, Duncan, BC Canada V9L 5Z2

About the Author

Henry Landry, author, life coach, guide and teacher is at One with the temporary nature of life. His career path has followed three directions, his early and first career was as a Cook, Chef and Kitchen Manager for ten years. Starting a Consulting business, he was involved in Provincial [State], and Federal [National] politics for ten years as a candidate trainer and party organizer. He was also an Executive Assistant to several Cabinet Ministers. His third career having gone back to university as a "mature student" was to become a Life Skills Coach and Counselor. Semi-retired this continues to be his pathway in the present.

His *spiritual pathway* and one that enables him to be a balanced teacher of the Buddhist Law, is such that early in life the guardians and messengers of the universe sent him a mentor that was to change his life. *Edward Demic*, an Oblate Priest, who left the Roman Catholic Church after twenty five years, befriended him and told him he would not find the truth or the answers to his questions in the church, but that he should study philosophy. This lead him to eight years of study in the Western philosophies while pursuing his career and family life. His Christian studies include thirty years of study of the life of the Jewish messenger Jesus and the study of the Christian faith and its various denominations. He has studied both Hebrew and Muslim faiths. He studied the way of the Rosicrucians for several years then beginning his study of the Eastern philosophies in his early thirties he took up the Yogic Pathways.

Next, he studied the provisional *Therevada* Buddhist doctrine. Then the Buddha Way appeared again, this time in the *Mahayana* tradition with the teachings of the Buddha of the Latter Day of the Law *Nichiren Daishonin* and Guatama Shakyamuni's *Lotus Sutra*.

Since 1985 he has lead a life of Nichiren Buddhist faith, practice and study. Healthy and happy in the beginning of the Winter of his life, he enjoys the love of family and friends, and many seekers of Buddhist Enlightenment. A Mahayana Nichiren Buddhist Teacher [Ajari] since 1995, he is dedicated to assisting others seek their highest self in the discovery of their very special human and Buddha nature.